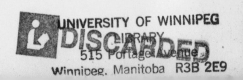

Britain Speaks

Books by
J. B. PRIESTLEY

FICTION

Let the People Sing · The Doomsday Men · They Walk in the City · Faraway · Angel Pavement · The Good Companions · Wonder Hero · Benighted Adam in Moonshine

PLAYS

Johnson Over Jordan · When We Are Married · Bees on the Boat Deck Duet in Floodlight · Cornelius · Eden End · Dangerous Corner · Laburnum Grove · The Roundabout

MISCELLANEOUS

Rain Upon Godshill · Midnight on the Desert · English Journey · Four-in-Hand · I for One · Talking: An Essay · Open House · Apes and Angels Self-Selected Essays · The Balconinny · The English Comic Characters Meredith (English Men of Letters) · Peacock (English Men of Letters) · The English Novel · Humour (English Heritage Series) · Brief Diversions

BRITAIN
SPEAKS

By

J. B. PRIESTLEY

HARPER & BROTHERS *Publishers*

New York *and* London

This story is published in England
under the title of POSTSCRIPTS

CONTENTS

[v]

CONTENTS

[vi]

CONTENTS

Britain Speaks

I. Civilization Can Defend Itself as Fiercely as Barbarism Can Attack

May 30, 1940

I'VE BEEN spending the last few days in my house in the country, only a few miles from the south coast. At odd times we've heard a sound like the distant banging of doors, which was, of course, the noise of bombs and anti-aircraft guns. It hasn't worried anybody very much. At the Star Inn just down the road, the regular customers in the taproom, sitting over their half pints of bitter, have been telling each other that we've all to set about stopping this Hitler. We've formed a local detachment of local defence volunteers or parashots, and I've joined them myself, but so far I've not been called on to take a turn at nightwatching on the downs. It's not the first time men have kept guard on these downs, for they did it in Queen Elizabeth's time and then in Napoleon's. And everybody's as cool as a cucumber. The Italians are saying, I read, that we're in a terrible panic, but all I can reply to that is that I've seen and heard more fuss and excitement just landing my luggage in Naples than I've seen and heard here since the war started. Not that we don't see anything.

Today I saw a train load of our troops just back from Flanders. They were unshaven; their faces were drawn and sunken-eyed; they had just been fighting one of the greatest rear-guard actions in modern history; they had been bombed day and night; but they were still giving us the thumbs-up sign. They looked what they were, undefeated, pushed back for a while by an overwhelming superiority of machines and armaments, but with no respect whatever for the hordes of robots using those machines and armaments.

Later today I had a long talk with an officer who had just returned from the northern battlefront. He was a man of my own generation, who like myself had been all through the last war, and so I was especially interested in what he had to say. The unit he commanded was not really a fighting unit at all, being composed of searchlights. Nevertheless his men, being asked to hold a bridge near a coast town, found themselves attacked by a motorised German detachment including three tanks, fought them there for five solid hours, and then beat them off. This officer, though admitting the ferocity of the attack of the German air force, which hardly ever stayed to fight our own airmen, but of course greatly outnumbered them, had nothing but a cold contempt for these Nazi troops, who, he said, were far worse types than the German soldiers of the last war.

Of all the things that have happened so far in this war, this deliberate harrying and destruction of refugees must rank as the greatest and foulest crime, and our own soldiers, who are if anything too easy-going and very hard to rouse, grow white with anger when they remember these atrocities. It has been, of course, a deliberate policy, just as much part of the planned invasion as the movements of airplanes and tanks. Just as the Red Indians often used to stampede herds of wild buffalo before they attacked, in order to disturb and hamper their enemies, so the Nazi strategists have deliberately stampeded and slaughtered refugees simply in order to create confusion, havoc and panic.

I don't want to dwell upon the horror of all this. The world gets plenty of that. But I do want to point out the significance of this vast crime. For it means that the Nazis have abandoned their last pretence of being a more or less civilised European power that had entered into a conflict with other European powers. If they imagined for a moment that they could be a member of the commonwealth of powers, they would never have dared to adopt such hellish tactics. The fact that they adopted them shows that the mask is off, that no compromise is possible with civilisation, that now either they will be destroyed or they will dominate the world. They themselves have furnished the best proof to everybody that this cannot possibly be regarded as just another quarrel among European powers; that now it is a fight to the death between the old civilisation of Christendom and this new evil empire of machines and robots.

There is a good letter from an American living in England that appeared in this morning's *Daily Telegraph*. He says that he refused to take his Embassy's advice to leave this country, and then goes on to add:

"Americans leaving England at this critical time are

deserting their own cause—Freedom and Liberty. The American frontier is the English Channel."

Well, that's what one American says. For my part, though I agree with him, I'd put it a bit differently. I'd say that this isn't a war in the old sense at all. It isn't a quarrel between certain nations. It isn't a matter of frontiers or possessions. It's a desperate battle, in which the whole future of the world is involved, between two ways of life. We don't say that one of them, ours, is perfect. We know very well it isn't. In fact some of us have spent a lot of our time these last few years criticising the sort of life we were leading. But at least it was worth criticising. Left to ourselves we could improve it, as we were improving it all the time, to give every man, woman and child a chance to lead a full, useful, and happy existence. But the other kind of life, which has spread like a foul stain over half Europe, is simply evil. It isn't German. There isn't a great German of the past who would not have indignantly refused to have any part in it, just as those great Germans of today have all turned their backs on it and are now in exile. It is simply a gigantic insane gangsterism, a vast power machine built for nothing but brutal conquest. You can't come to terms with it. There's no living peacefully alongside it, because it has no intention of living peacefully itself or of allowing you to live at peace. It is no more simply European than typhoid fever is simply European, and like a plague, if it is not stopped here, then it will spread all over the world.

But of course it isn't going to be allowed to spread. What is the position at the moment? The battle of the north still continues. Further south and east, the French, along with the other section of the British Expeditionary Force, is holding the line of the Somme and strengthening their defence. Here at home we are at last—and of course as usual it is "at last"—going into strict training for the big fight.

In my opinion, for what it's worth, we've probably done more to make ourselves really fit and ready in the last three weeks than we did in the previous eight months. One reason for the delay is that you can't persuade a lot of the English that they don't live on a magic island. They believe, these nice comfortable stupid folk, that disasters and tragedies, fire and slaughter, treachery and invasion, are things that only happen over the sea, to those strange excitable beings called "foreigners." It's only a month or two ago that the girl who works in our kitchen said quite solemnly, "Does this man Hitler realise what trouble and expense he's putting us to?" The answer is that he does, and likes it. But that was the attitude of mind of many of the English up to a few weeks ago. But now that's gone. Not only because the war has been brought nearer these shores, but also I think, because the people feel that this new government of ours means business, that its leaders are determined vital men. There's none of that sleepy complacency any more.

The temper of the ordinary easy-going English folk

is rising. Any attempt at invasion will only send it up a few more degrees. I haven't met anybody yet who's particularly worried about it. Naturally when your whole world changes so rapidly, it isn't easy to make the necessary adjustments. I know it's tough going trying to be an author these days, for you can't settle down to write a book, the theatres are closing, not because people are afraid to go to them but partly because they want to listen to the news at night and also they like to get a bit of fresh air after a long day indoors, and even journalism has been cut down. But I for one am in better trim physically than I was a year ago, I'm no worse mentally, and it'll certainly do me no harm taking my turn on the downs watching the searchlights sweeping the sky and looking out for parachute troops. I only hope they don't come down in our part all dressed as clergymen, because I have a feeling our chaps are going to be very embarrassed chasing every clergyman they see. You know, all this business is the most tragic thing that's ever happened to us—it seems far more tragic to me than the last war, though I was only young then and a soldier—but in spite of it all, you find yourself laughing still, there's a lot of absurdity about, as there always will be in this absurd, beautiful and lovable island of ours. And that's something the Germans will never understand. They don't understand us when we laugh, they don't understand us when we're serious. And they won't learn. They'll never never learn. But there's a strong feeling about—I read it not in the newspapers but in the

[6]

faces of all the folks I see—and I hear it in their voices—that very soon they'll be taught one or two things they haven't quite understood yet. One of them is that civilisation can defend itself as fiercely as barbarism can attack, and can continue to do it, can keep it up, with more patience, for patience, like truth-telling and kindness, are civilised virtues.

II. Never Have We Seen or
Enjoyed So Lovely a Spring

June 5, 1940

THE SECOND great battle has begun, and this time in a far more orthodox fashion than the first, with waves of infantry instead of masses of tanks. It is extraordinary how the same old names, familiar during the last war and many a war before that, keep cropping up again—Abbéville, Peronne, Amiens. It was through a ruined Peronne that I travelled when I went up to the front line for the last time—I had been there twice before, in 1915 and 1916—through the dust and heat of early September, 1918, and when I returned, a casualty again, I was taken through Amiens, to be attended to afterwards, by the way, by an American doctor. We ought to have known that no matter where this war started it would soon return to the old front lines, to that terrible region of the Somme, where in July 1916 so many of my fellow townsmen perished that there was hardly left one man whom I had known as a boy. If there are ghosts, then millions of them must be watching this battle now. And we, who are not yet ghosts and indeed feel very much alive, are all watching it too. English troops are in action there, but here at home we are now making a tremendous effort to strengthen all defence against invasion, so that as soon as possible we can augment our forces in France, for a military defeat for the Germans there means the end of Hitler, just as it meant the end of the Kaiser and Ludendorff in 1918.

So we are rapidly turning this island of ours into the greatest fortress the world has ever known. We are working fast. Temperamentally we may be averse to making elaborate long-range plans, and therefore we always begin at a disadvantage when we are faced with an enemy like the cunning and methodical Germans, who set to work to dominate the world years in advance of their first open move, toiling like ants and termites. But on the other hand, we have the gift of rapid and effective improvisation, as we have just seen in the magnificent embarkation at Dunkirk. And now we are applying that gift to the defence of this island. More has been done during the last week than was done during the last hundred years. People who might turn out to be Fifth Columnists have been rounded up by the hundred. If parachute troops are landed here they're going to find themselves a bit lonely and not among friends. Children have been evacuated from towns on the east and south-east coast. Even the sheep and cattle are being moved from some coastal districts. Strategic areas have been mined. There are hundreds and hundreds of concrete and sandbagged machine-guns posts. All public buildings are guarded. Two men were shot by a sentry the other day when they refused to halt at his command. Large flat open spaces are now our danger points, because troop-carrying planes could be landed on them,

and now they are being dug up and wired so that landing is impossible. Even race-courses—those hallowed
stretches of turf—are being roughly handled in this
fashion.

This of course is only the beginning, for I can hardly
begin to suggest the thousand-and-one precautions that
are being taken. The parashot corps, which is functioning everywhere, now numbers over four hundred thousand. In addition there are the various home defence
services, and now we are to have the Ironsides, General
Ironside's new creation, a corps of picked regular soldiers, very mobile and heavily armed. This corps will
be specially trained to deal quickly with enemy troops
suddenly landed by air or sea. They will, I prophesy
here and now, be a tough crowd, and more than a match
for any half-doped young fanatics that Goering shovels
out of his airplanes. And England will prove a very
awkward country for an enemy to manoeuvre in. It's a
very different proposition from Northern France and
Flanders, with their long straight roads, without hedges
and ditches, along which motorised units can roar at full
speed because they can see miles ahead. Here we have,
as Chesterton said in his poem, "the rolling English
road," which goes this way and then that, seems to turn
back on itself, and meanders all over the place, with
ditches and hedges everywhere for cover. I don't care
how good the German maps of England are, how clever
their staff work, they will soon find themselves lost and
tangled if they ever do succeed in landing a force of

any size, for every sign has been removed from these mazes of winding roads and lanes, and we're beginning to be lost ourselves if we travel too far from home. And God help anybody who asks the way in a thick German accent. This morning, coming up from the country, I passed half a dozen stout barricades within ten miles of my house.

As an example of what can happen to an enemy from the sky there is the adventure of my friend Ralph Richardson, the actor. He's a pilot now and not long ago he was compelled to make a forced landing on a village green not far from the South Coast. The villagers thought it must be a German plane masquerading as one of ours. But did they run away? They did not. They came charging on with scythes and shovels, and it was lucky for Ralph that he was a film star and so easily recognised. I like to think of those village men who, machine gun or no machine gun, were ready to take a crack at anybody who thought he could drop from the sky on them.

It takes an awful lot to rouse the ordinary English folk. They're apt to be an easy, sleepy, good-natured crowd, but once they are roused—and the terrible tales of mass murder brought back by the B.E.F. are doing that—they'll wade in and never stop. You know how it is with a bulldog—he'll let you tease him and maul him about perhaps for an hour or two, but go an inch too far and he'll sink his teeth into you and never let go. Well, that's the real English, the ordinary quiet folk. They aren't saying much—the "chatterbug," as the defeatist gossiper is called, is a special type, and there are very few of them among the ordinary working folk—but believe me, they're solidly behind every word that Mr. Churchill uttered in his great speech yesterday. And the nearer the Nazis get, the more that slow but dogged temper is going to rise.

A lot of the stuff heard over the air or read in the press about the British public is based on what goes on in London West End clubs or Mayfair restaurants, where you'll often find plenty of dismal Jimmies and "chatterbugs." But if you want to know what the ordinary folk are thinking and feeling here, you've got to go into the workshops or the pubs, especially the little taverns in the small towns and villages, and when you find those men looking long-faced and repeating the rubbish invented by German propaganda, then it's time to begin worrying. And I haven't found a trace of it yet. The people are glad now to have a government that'll pile some responsibility on them and set them to work and to fight.

Since this war began many thoughtful and generous American friends have written to me offering to take the children in my family and look after them until the war was over. Others all the way from New York to San Francisco have told me how often they're thinking about us and feeling sorry for us here. While I thank them, I also want to say this. Now that the real blitzkrieg has begun, and all hell is let loose, I feel sorrier for these friends in their position than I do for us in ours. And I'll tell you exactly why. If my American friends lived in another world altogether, where they'd never even heard of what's happening here, then I might envy them. But they do not. They're three thousand miles away, but what does that mean in these days? All the news of these treacheries and mass murders, this hell-upon-earth that one maniac has created, reaches my American friends just as quickly as it reaches us here. And like us, they're pouncing on the latest editions of the newspapers, they're for ever turning on the radio to listen breathlessly to the very last reports from the front. Like us, these American friends of mine can't really think about anything else but these invasions and bombings and wholesale slaughter. Confronted by these disasters and threats to the whole civilised world, they can no more get on with their ordinary lives than we can get on with ours. Only there is this difference. Though my American friends feel all the horror and anguish of this time, just as we do, they are really worse off in mind and spirit now than we are, because they can only stare at the dreadful scene in terror and pity, like people on the seashore who watch a great ship struggling against a terrible storm. But we, who are on the ship and in the storm, are now so completely engrossed in action that there comes to us, as a compensation for all our effort, a certain feeling of expansion, a heightening of the spirit, a sense that somewhere in this struggle of free men against drilled and doped slaves there is a moral grandeur. Soon, some of us may die, but nobody can say of us now that we are not alive, and it is a fact that while one disaster piles upon another many of us have told each other that never have we seen or enjoyed so lovely a Spring.

So I say, do not pity us.

After talking to our boys just back from Dunkirk I have been remembering the famous saying of Henry the Fourth of France, when he met the friend of his who had missed the great battle. He said: "Go hang yourself, brave Crillon. We fought at Arques, and you were not there." But now all of us here are fighting at Arques.

III. A Cross-section of Opinion

June 7, 1940

I'VE HAD to spend most of today going about central London on one errand and another. So I thought it would be interesting to ask various people of all types what they were thinking and feeling about the war, and I believe I've got a good and honest cross-section of London opinion.

For instance, this morning I had to visit my tailor, so I asked the chief cutter, who's a solemn ecclesiastical-looking fellow, what he felt about the war. He replied: "I have infinite faith, sir, in the ability of our French Allies to defend their native soil, and as for us, sir, we are unconquerable."

He always looks very earnest—a sort of high priest of men's wear—but when he made this reply he managed to look even ten times more earnest than ever, and nearly frightened me.

Then having to call on a friend in business, I asked his secretary, a fairly typical London bachelor girl, what she was feeling about it all. She said, very seriously: "In the end we shall win, but we shall have a hell of a time first."

This girl, by the way, after doing a long day's work in her office acts as an air-raid warden in her particular suburb, and so is liable to be called out at all hours of the night. No joke that.

[15]

Next, after buying a newspaper or two, I asked the man who was selling them to give me his opinion. He grinned, but nevertheless he took the question quite seriously. "It's going to be all right," he said, "and it never did worry me."

He had a pal there, a much older man, one of those toothless Cockneys with pushed-in faces. "And what about you?" I asked him.

He said, "Same as him only a size larger." Nothing defeatist about that pair.

Moving on again, I called on an old friend, an elderly business man of very great ability. "Now tell me," I said, "*exactly* what you think."

He thought for a moment, then replied: "Well, I'm disgusted at the muddle we've been in right up to now. We'll win, but we hardly deserve to."

I asked him to explain whom he meant by that "we" who hardly deserved to win, and said that surely he didn't mean the ordinary English people. He admitted that he didn't—the ordinary people were all right, and had been right from the first—but the crowd that annoyed him were the officials, the departmental mandarins, the Whitehall pundits, for whom, as a very efficient man himself, he had no respect whatever.

With this point of view I must confess I have some sympathy. Since this war began I've travelled thousands and thousands of miles in this country and talked to people of all kinds, and I must say I never saw much wrong with their attitude. They were nearly all only too eager to get on with the war, to do everything in their power to help their country, and were told too often there was nothing they could do and that everything was going on swimmingly without them. Which, as we know now, was simply not true; not that the bland official persons who said such things were deliberately deceiving the public—but they had not grasped the full reality of the situation, and were busy underestimating the energy and ruthless drive of the enemy.

This friend of mine, by the way, told me that he had just had a visit from an old acquaintance, a man of sixty-eight, who had applied to the government for the most dangerous job that could be found—looking after a dump of high explosives that might go off at any moment. He had said to them: "Look here, I'm sixty-eight and haven't much longer to go anyhow. Give me one of those really dangerous jobs and so take it away from some young man who's got his life in front of him." I wonder what'll happen to that brave old boy.

I am reminded by this that a member of parliament, Sir Arnold Wilson, is reported missing and believed to be killed in active service. Now I didn't know Sir Arnold Wilson, but during the two years before the war, when we were all bitterly quarrelling about our foreign policy, I looked upon him as a type of the dangerous extreme right-wing Tory who apparently admired the Nazi regime and wanted us to come to an understanding with Hitler. He was to my mind then—

and I haven't changed it since, of course—one of the people whose views were a real menace to democracy. But several months ago he said, "I am now convinced that the issue between Germany and England must be fought out to a finish." At the age of fifty-five, and after going through the last war, he joined the Air Force, was trained as a gunner, and is now "missing, believed killed." Honour where honour is due: there went a brave man. And when I read about Wilson, I began to wonder if it wasn't time I was back again into uniform— as I'll be glad to be when I'm wanted, though God knows that after spending years earning my living by speaking my mind I have a suspicion now that the army would soon court-martial me for persistent answering back and insolence to superior officers.

But to return to today. This afternoon I had some shopping to do, and so carried my question about the war into shops. One young woman who manages, very successfully, a large bookshop, replied that in her opinion the English can't be beaten. She didn't say this complacently, as some of our unimaginative older people are apt to do, but said it with a simple but profound air of conviction. I think what she meant was not that she belonged to a nation that was ever victorious, but that she felt in her heart—as I do in mine—that there is something in our nature that will not allow us to be beaten, that is, to have our will broken, our spirit of resistance completely destroyed, that if necessary we will die but we will never *give in*.

Let me say once again that the ordinary English folk

tend to be slack, sleepy, easy-going, chiefly because they have taken their security for granted, but that once they are really roused they can rise to astonishing heights of courage, endurance and sacrifice. In the last war every time this country was bombed, the recruiting figures jumped up at once; and every bomb that falls here now will raise and not lower the public morale. Mind you, flesh-and-blood can only stand so much; but so long as we've machines to fight back, and the promise of more to make the numbers a bit more even, then these people of ours can take anything that Goering can give them. And there's another thing to remember. Our people—unlike Goering's people—were never promised complete immunity from bombing. It is not the English but the German civilians who were bamboozled and coddled by impossible promises of this kind. Our people haven't to be kept going, month by month, by being assured that some colossal victory, with medals and triumphant marches and bells ringing, is round every corner. Every time Mr. Churchill talks to his people he does something that hasn't happened in public in Germany for years—he tells the truth.

But let me get back to my shopping this afternoon. One assistant, a man this time, replied to my question by saying thoughtfully that he was confident we should win but that it would take another two years or so.

It's funny about shops here. They're still crammed with goods, perhaps too full, for I feel that we could now dispense with a lot of the luxury articles. I wish we could send a few cargoes of these fine luxury things of ours across the Atlantic in exchange for some good fast planes. About one shop out of every four in any English town sells chocolates and sweets or—as Americans call it—candy. And there they all are, to this very day, stuffed to the roof. Why, in the last war, I can remember walking miles and miles, searching all over the place, just for one little box of chocolates to give some girl I was taking out for the evening—this was when I was on leave from the front—and I can remember how triumphant I'd feel when at last I'd manage to find and buy some fly-blown little box of inferior stuff, and with what a grand air I'd produce it and hand it over to the girl friend. Now, there's still tons of this sweet stuff down every shopping street, and I don't believe those young soldiers now walk miles and miles in search of any present.

Their girl friends, incidentally, are now becoming very feminine. When the war began all the girls—and, alas for their appearance, a great many women who ought to have been old enough to know better—rushed into trousers. Wearing trousers seemed to some of these women to be itself a wonderful kind of war work. But now, with real battle round the corner, the men are beginning to assert themselves—or the girls are obeying their more profound intuitions—and the trousers are disappearing, flowered and frilly skirts are returning to charm and captivate the warrior males.

Regent Street and Oxford Street this afternoon were packed with shoppers, chiefly women. I noticed, though, in the shops I had to deal with, that most of the assistants were middle-aged and very busy—and, like all of us, a trifle absent-minded. It's not that they didn't get on with their work—we're all doing that, and as a matter of fact some of our war industries have reached a pace of production beyond anything ever achieved here before— but that these assistants would forget some little thing and then have to jog themselves. I find it just the same. The mind is like an automobile that's running on four cylinders instead of its full six. We keep remembering that one of the world's great battles—for all we know the most decisive battle in history—is being fought not two hundred miles away.

Our minds all work rather oddly now. I had to laugh at myself, the other day. On the top of my house in the country I have a study with unusually large windows. It occurred to me, just after we'd heard some bombing and firing in the night, that it was about time I made these windows safe. So I stuck long strips of brown paper over them, making pretty patterns, and as I did it I began grumbling to myself, saying that this was bad enough, but what an awful laborious business it would be scraping all these strips off the windows, and what a horrible nuisance I would find it. And then I remembered—and had to laugh at myself—for I suddenly saw that when the time comes for those strips of paper to be scraped off the windows I shan't mind doing it at all, for it will mean that the war will be over, that the shadow that has been darkening the civilised world for years will have disappeared, and that we can all come out into the sun again.

IV. A Night on Duty with
the Parashots

June 14, 1940

THE FALL of Paris, an event of greater symbolical than purely military significance, has produced some very marked reactions here in London, its sister city. The average man has been assured over and over again during these last few days that our Government is giving France every scrap of assistance possible, and we know how men and munitions and machines are being rushed across the Channel. No considerations of home defence are being allowed to stand in the way of these new forces and supplies, for nobody doubts that while France still holds out so magnificently, our front line, the front line of all the democracies, is over there. But the fall of Paris—the world's city of light and laughter and art—has now increased the demands, now made by press and public alike, that more men here should be enlisted at once; that new armies of older men should be instantly formed and begin drilling; that if equipment for such new armies is still lacking, as it was in the army I joined in 1914, then that should not be allowed to stand in the way; that men should be drilled in public parks with broomsticks rather than left, helpless and exasperated, in civilian life.

Hundreds of thousands of men here feel that really

they have already said goodbye to civilian life, and all they ask is for some acquaintance with military training and weapons to be put into their hands. They feel that they cannot remain outside the giant battle any longer. Hitler's hordes must be stopped. There is more than one way of stopping them. So now I want to take you on duty with me for the night with our local defence volunteers, or parashots.

The place of meeting and sentry post is on top of a down, with a fine view almost in every direction, extending over a dozen parishes. It is nearly dusk. Far away is a last glimmer of the sea. There are more men at the post than will be wanted on duty, simply because the local men have got into the habit of strolling up to the post just before dusk to smoke a pipe and have a crack with their fellow volunteers. Some are in uniform —it looks not unlike the battle dress of the regular soldiers but is more an overall than a suit—and most of these wear ribbons showing that they were in the last war. A few are not yet in uniform, and so wear an arm-let. There are some old but quite serviceable army rifles and ball cartridges, for the men going on duty. Ours is a small but scattered village, and practically every able-bodied man in it takes his turn at this night duty.

The men I met the other night represented a good cross-section of English rural life. The man in charge was a farm bailiff who had been in the last war. Then there was the engineer from the local brick works; there was a builder; there was the parson; there was a woodman; there was a carrier; there was a shepherd; there was a hurdle-maker, and of course several farmers and farm labourers. Their preliminary talk about planes they had observed on recent nights, during which there had been several raids not very far away, gave the whole horrible business of air raids a sort of comfortable rustic atmosphere, and really made a man feel more cheerful about it.

As is their manner, they called every plane "she." They would say: "Ay, she come along thru the gap an' over along by Little Witchett—as I see with my own eyes. Then searchloights picks her up—moight be Black Chine way or further along, over by Colonel Wilson's may be—an' oi says to Tarm, oi says 'Won't be long noow, you'll see, afore they gets her'—an' then —by Christmas—she trois to doive—an' Tarm says 'She's troing to give them searchlight boys a bit o' machine-gun work, see?'—an' I says to Tarm 'Won't be long afore they gets her, you'll see'—an' then—bingo, masters, down she comes, moines an' all, an' fair shook the whole plaace."

You might think they were describing a bit of beagling or dry-fly fishing. They were being quite serious and sincere about it all, but their sound rustic habit of relating everything intimately to their own familiar background, though it did not take away any of the real menace, did somehow put all this raiding and invading in their proper places, represented them not as the lunatic end of everything but as the latest manifestation of that everlasting menace the countryman has to fight, along with sudden blizzards at lambing time or floods just before the harvest. And as we talked we watched the dusk deepen in the valleys below, saw our fading houses, farms and cottages, where our women folk were listening to the news on the wireless as they knitted socks and scarves for the soldiers and sailors, and remembered that these were our homes and that now at any time they might be blazing ruins.

The sentries took their posts. Those who weren't on duty, or who had to guard places away from the hilltop, now left us. There was mist coming in from the sea. Nothing much happened for a time. A green light that seemed to defy all the black-out regulations turned out to be merely an extra-large and unusually luminous glow-worm that had attached itself to a gate a few feet away. A few searchlights went stabbing through the dusk for a few moments, and then faded. They were merely being tested. Above, the mist thickened, and below, in all the valley, there was not the faintest glimmer of light. Without failing to keep an eye and an ear alert, we talked in an easy rambling style—about what happened to us in the last war, about the hay and the barley, about the land girls who were now arriving in these parts, about beef and milk and cheese and tobacco, but, curiously enough, hardly at all about the war in general.

One sentry—Bill by name and gawky by nature—kept reporting lights that the rest of us could not see and

sounds that we could not hear, and always he turned out
to be right; not to be merely nervous, as at first I judged
him to be, but to have senses far more acute than the
rest of us had. The truth is, that Bill has spent many
and many a night poaching—creeping about the woods
with his gun when the rest of us were asleep. And
though I realise that we volunteers cannot hope to
withstand trained troops armed with machine-guns, I
cannot help feeling that chaps like Bill, who know every
inch of the local countryside, who have eyes like hawks,
who can keep still under cover, who are very good shots,
may prove awkward opponents for these young men
who drop on us from the skies. It was he who, some
time after midnight, when nothing had happened for
ages, it seemed, and we were all rather disappointed,
told us there were planes about. For some time the rest
of us couldn't hear the faintest throb. All we could hear
was the ceaseless high melancholy singing of the telegraph wires in the wind. But then a belt of sea-fog over
to the left began to lighten and become almost silvery,
not because it was breaking but because somewhere along
there dozens of searchlights were sweeping the sky.
Then somewhere behind that vague silveriness, it was
as if gigantic doors were being hastily shut. After a few
minutes more this distant door-slamming had changed
to something nearer and more menacing, a kind of dull
crump-crump, almost as much a vast shiver as a sound.
Then the rapid stabbing noise of anti-aircraft batteries,
with some rapping, blanketed a little by the mist, of

machine-guns. A few more *crump-crumps*. Then a few minutes' silence. This silence was broken, most dramatically, by the unexpected noise of the sirens in our two nearest towns. It was as if all that part of the darkened countryside, like a vast trapped animal, was screaming at us.

I will confess that I detest these horrible high wailing sirens; in the last war we used maroons—that is, loud explosive signals—as air-raid warnings, and it is a pity we don't return to them. But there they went, and we heard and watched from our hill-top. I should like to describe to you now great shattering explosions, flames a thousand feet high, planes toppling and crashing like grouse in August, horrors upon horrors, but I am a truthful man and so must confess that after the sirens went nothing of any consequence happened at all. The sounds of bombs and gunfire and the hum of planes all died away. There was nothing but the misty cool night, lost in silence, and this handful of us on the hill-top. I felt up there a very powerful and rewarding sense of community. And with it too a sense of deep continuity. Ploughman or parson, shepherd or author, we were Englishmen, turning out at night, as our fore-fathers had often done before us, to keep watch and ward over the sleeping English hills and fields and homes. We laugh at ourselves, we volunteers, but please don't you laugh at us. For remember whenever these men will be called upon to take action, it is more than likely that the odds will be against them. Moreover, even now, they come to these long night watches after a heavy day's work in the fields or workshops, for all of them must work now much harder than they ever did before—these country folk are at it from daylight—and to be out in the night too is no joke. And if the armies in France don't hold, then here there may very well soon be all the shattering explosions, the blazing farm-steads, the ruined towns, the horrors piled upon horrors, that those newspaper readers seemed to want when they called this "a phoney war."

We have not yet been called upon to perform those miracles of endurance and courage that the French population is performing, but the hour draws ever nearer, and while there is yet time we are now hurling all our energies into the task of helping our Allies and defending ourselves. Even this house of mine in the country, which used to ring with the voices and laughter of our children, is now silent, with never a child near it. Like hundreds of thousands of other women here, my wife, who runs a Red Cross depot, a first-aid post, helps with the local A.R.P., and in between times works in the garden, is busy from morning till night, and tries vainly to pretend that she is not missing the children. Our life of a year ago, when we were in London giving and going to parties, now seems like some dim old dream. And of June next year we do not think at all, for at these times we can only live from week to week.

That is how it is with us, the British. With the French, it is even more desperate. They must think, they must

live, they must work and battle, only from day to day.
And how these lines of verse come home today!

O star! O ship of France, beat back and baffled long!
Bear up, O smitten orb! O ship continue on.
Again thy star, O France, fair lustrous star,
In heavenly peace, clearer, more bright than ever,
Shall beam immortal.

Those lines, which might have been composed for
today, were actually written many many years ago, and
by an American poet—Walt Whitman.

V. The Issue Is Plain—We Can't
Live with Nazism

June 15, 1940

O N THIS day, exactly seven hundred and twenty-five years ago, the hostile barons assembled on the meadow at Runnymede, laid their Forty-eight Articles before King John, and forced him to accept them. The result was Magna Carta, that great charter which is one of the instruments and examples, the first of them, of the peculiar political genius of the Anglo-Saxon people, a genius that crossed the Atlantic to establish new and still greater commonwealths of free peoples.

The high road that our people reached at Magna Carta is the high road that we are all on to this day, and now we find it blocked by the most sinister, menacing and totally destructive power known to modern history. That power is the avowed enemy of all that you and I care about. If we don't destroy it, then it will destroy us. These aren't mere phrases, they're the sober truth. I don't believe the American people can share a world with Nazism, especially a triumphant all-conquering Nazism, and even if they wanted to—and I'm sure they don't—they wouldn't be allowed to. This is not a European struggle. It is a world conflict or it is nothing. You notice that Hitler is now saying that to suppose that he has any designs on the new world is absurd and grotesque. By this time, we ought to have realised that once Hitler has said a thing like that, his mind is really moving in the opposite direction. He told us that he had no designs on Czechoslovakia, Poland, Norway, Holland, Belgium, and where are they now? Under the iron boots of the storm troopers and the Gestapo. A great many people in the new world are now repeating the mistakes that we made a year ago—they're imagining that you can stop Hitler by holding a meeting and passing a resolution to say you don't approve of him. As if he cared! Why, nobody ever approved of him. He's raised himself to this stupendous altitude of power on this kind of woolly well-meaning ineffectual disapproval.

Well, we're long past that here now. We've made our usual mistakes. We've been too complacent; we've underestimated the enormous preparation and ruthlessness of the enemy; we've depended too long on a gentlemanly slow-motion civil-service system, which couldn't key up our war industries to the proper pitch. But now that's gone. The real English people, not a small ruling class, are now taking charge, led by men like Bevin, Morrison, Greenwood. We're producing planes and munitions at a rate that far exceeds anything ever known before in this island. The pace is becoming terrific. And nothing Hitler can do, short of over-running the whole country, can stop it.

The issue is plain. We simply can't live with Nazism. Either we destroy it or it destroys us. And I don't believe it can destroy us. We have behind us the resources of a vast empire. While Hitler is throwing into the battle everything he's got, we're only just getting into our stride. Nobody's going to pretend it'll be easy, for you can't defy the most enormous and devilish mechanism of destruction the world has ever seen and expect to be on velvet. We realise that now. It's not a pretty prospect. A lot of us may be maimed or dead very soon, but that can't be helped. We'll go on and on until we break their black hearts. Whatever the Nazis may say, this is still an island. No endless procession of heavy tanks is going to roll in here, as they did over the straight flat roads of Flanders. Mussolini was reported as saying, a few years ago, that now in these days of air forces, the British Navy was just so much old scrap iron. I'll bet he isn't saying that now, and I'll take another bet that very soon he'll wish he'd never been so foolish as to say it. Of course they've got a trick or two up their sleeves, but perhaps our sleeves aren't empty either, only we're not making a fuss about it.

Now what's the position at the moment? Hitler, by sacrificing men and machines as no commander ever sacrificed them before, has reached Paris, and no doubt will soon have a fine goose-stepping parade there, which no doubt will compensate the Germans for the million casualties that they haven't heard about yet. But the fact remains that the world is closing round him—the entrance of Italy into the war has only shut another big door, through which supplies had been pouring since last September—whereas the world is wide open to us. Napoleon, a far greater man than Hitler, closed the whole continent of Europe to England, and declared that we were done for, but a few years afterwards it was he who was done for, and Britain was triumphant. Do the Nazis know all this? Of course they do, and their whole policy is based on that knowledge. It is based too on another kind of knowledge, namely, an amazing capacity for guessing at the weaknesses and timidities of other people and making full use of them. They have succeeded far more by guessing accurately at other people's weaknesses than by establishing their own strength. Remember this about them—for it is their secret—that they don't, as the rest of us tend to do, separate warfare, diplomacy, espionage, into different departments, but they keep them all moving along together. If they aren't attacking with their armoured columns, then they're attacking with their fifth columns, spreading rumours, encouraging those weaknesses and timidities.

Hitler has no interest in America, eh? Then why all the elaborate network of espionage in the United States? The Nazis don't spend money and take time and trouble on something in which they're not interested. If they've gone to the trouble and expense of establishing their agents throughout an enormous territory, you may be sure they are making good use of those agents. Why has Hitler chosen this time to say that he has no interest in the western world? Because this is the very time when he has the greatest possible interest in the western world. He knows that the pace of his recent drives is as unendurable to his own people as it is to the forces they have swept back, that even his own severely disciplined and fantastically deluded people cannot keep

[33]

this up much longer, that the thought of another winter, with the blockade still tightening and all supplies vanishing, is a nightmare. Why is it that both Hitler and Mussolini concentrate on our sea power as our most insufferable and challenging possession? If that sea power were unimportant, as they like to pretend when they're being boastful, then they'd be completely indifferent about it, and think us fools for spending so much on such extravagant useless toys as battleships. But they know very well that that line of strong grey ships, still unbroken, whether in the North Sea, the Mediterranean, the Atlantic, is like a rope round their necks, and that slowly but surely it is tightening, tightening. While that great Navy exists, and there stands behind it a united people, only toughened by reverses on land, all their talk of vast empires, in which millions and millions of serfs will work for the "master race," is only a pipe dream.

VI. Lord Woolton and the Food Situation

June 21, 1940

NOBODY doubts now that during the first six months of this war, the Allies—and indeed nearly all the rest of the world—seriously and most dangerously underestimated the military power of the Nazis. It was not realised that they could strike so suddenly and with so gigantic a weight of arms. I notice now, however, an opposite but equally dangerous tendency—to over-estimate these same German forces, to imagine that they are irresistible, that nobody, nothing, can stand against them. With this I am in total disagreement, and as it is more than likely that the lives of my family and myself depend upon this judgment, you may be sure I haven't arrived at it lightly. I take the view that although the Nazi engine of war is extremely formidable, nevertheless there is about its activities and prestige, as there is about everything the Nazis do, except their police work, a certain definite, though not calculable, element of bluff; that now they have put all their goods in the front window, so to speak, and if they meet, what they haven't met yet, a stubborn, tough, protracted resistance, that machine of theirs will begin to show rapid signs of wear and tear, will begin to crack, and after a time may suddenly fall to pieces. I believe too that that is the kind of resistance they'll now get from us, from a people who are, whatever their faults, psychologically tougher and more naturally resourceful than the German.

Also, it is as well to bear in mind that Hitler and his staff are not sea-minded. Hitler, an untravelled Central European, really knows no more about the sea than a prairie dog, and I suspect that he is impatient with those who try to correct his ignorance and indifference. In 1810 Napoleon's rule extended from Northern Scandinavia to Southern Spain, it was wider in area than Hitler's, but for all that his continental blockade of Britain failed. Hitler will probably try a blitzkrieg version of the same thing, making full use of his submarines and planes, but I believe he will fail too. Which brings us to the food situation.

It is well known that the prospects in all parts of Western Europe are very bad indeed. The harvests will be unusually poor. Germany has been feeding her army and heavy workers on the loot of Denmark and the Low Countries, and now the larders of France will be robbed. But with the British blockade still tightening, this is a desperate business. The cattle and pigs of Denmark can be killed and eaten only once. The dairies of the Dutch can't be robbed over and over again. Meanwhile all these conquered people, who have been robbed in this fashion, will have to be fed somehow. You may be sure the Nazis will let them have as little as possible, but they will have to have something, otherwise very soon terrible diseases will break out and Germany will find itself besieged by plagues. Unfortunately it is difficult to help these populations, for—as we discovered in the last war—if you give Germany food for them, Germany does not pass on that food but uses it to feed her army. If it is possible soon to ensure that foodstuffs from the new world do actually reach these desperate folk, then so much the better. But the Nazis have a very lean winter to look forward to, and the fact that Italy was ordered to come in, thereby closing the last gateway through which any large amount of supplies reached Germany, suggests that Hitler is gambling on finishing the war before the winter.

I've been trying to decide lately whether my American friends are cleverer than other people's American friends or not so generous. You see, nearly all the people I know who have friends in America have been receiving from them parcels containing fine Virginia hams, nourishing slabs of chocolate, and other foodstuffs. And I haven't had a single parcel. True, I'm not in the slightest need of food parcels from America or anywhere else—nobody here is; you can eat yourself sick, if you want to—but of course it's very nice to have a parcel or two of America's noblest produce, including perhaps a bottle of rye or bourbon. As I can't believe my particular American friends are less generous than other people's, I can only conclude they must be better informed than other people's friends about conditions here. There is no shortage or signs of a shortage of essential foodstuffs in this country. There is not as much meat about as there used to be, but there is certainly far more than I want or need. I fancy a great many people here are much healthier than they were a year

ago. Of course, in a world as crazy as ours, with one
country after another affected by our blockade, and
with many normal trade routes and trade channels not
functioning regularly, it isn't easy to provision this
country properly. Now and then the housewife may
have had to worry, but on the whole so far it is the
Ministry of Food that has done the worrying, behind
the scenes, and has planned and schemed and organised
to some purpose. I was there only this morning, talking
to various people I knew in its vast warren of offices.

Our Ministry of Food is really the largest shop in
the world. It has fifteen hundred local food offices to
control supplies. It has eleven hundred meat depots. It
has over eight hundred local food depots, and each of
these local food depots has sufficient supplies to last
weeks and weeks and weeks even if completely isolated.
The Ministry has accumulated gigantic stocks of all
essential foodstuffs. It has a turnover of six hundred
million pounds sterling per annum. It imports nearly
ninety per cent. of all the foodstuffs that come into the
country. It has a staff of over twenty-three thousand
persons. It has saved the country millions of pounds by
buying great stocks of food supplies in all parts of the
world just at the moments when markets were ready to
sell. It has also deprived Germany of essential supplies.
Thus, just before the war it bought the whole whale oil
yield of Norway, beating Germany to it by sharp and
shrewd action. Not long ago it bought the whole sultana
crop of 1940, increased the use of sultanas by giving

the fruit wide publicity, and then cleared the whole
stock—with more than four million pounds—before any
of the fruit perished. It has a new milk scheme that
comes into operation on the first of next month, when
every expectant or nursing mother and every child under
five will get one pint of milk a day at half the market
price, and those who cannot afford this half-price will
receive their milk free.

The Minister of Food, with whom I had a long talk
this morning, is Lord Woolton. He is a husky man in
his late fifties, with a good big nose and a penetrating
eye. Like all people who are the salt of the earth, he
comes from the North of England. He does not belong
to the ruling or official class—thank God! His career
has been as curious as it has been successful. Originally
he was a lecturer in economics, and connected with various Northern universities. Then he went into business,
finally accepting an invitation to join the staff of Lewis's,
a big store in Liverpool, at first as director of labour
affairs. There he made good his theory that the right
policy was not to lower wages but to do more business
so as to make it possible to pay higher wages. Soon he
became managing director of the firm, which proceeded
to open branches in nearly every big provincial town.
Last summer he was called in to clothe the whole army—
named the day when he would have them all clothed,
and finished exactly one day before. He was able to do
this not only because he is a superb organiser and manager of men, but also because, unlike so many of our

men in high places here, he did not hesitate to cut through yards of red tape and refused to play the usual civil service game of passing on memoranda. His ministry is largely staffed by successful experts from the world of food business, and many of these men have left very responsible positions and large salaries to accept even quite subordinate places in the ministry. There is probably far more direct action and less official humbug—Circumlocution Office tactics—in the Ministry of Food than in any ministry we have. And Lord Woolton, having run big stores and having been compelled to study the public mind, believes in getting into direct contact with the public and not hiding himself behind some gigantic wall of hush-hush bureaucracy. He talks to our housewives over the radio, reassuring them about our stocks of food but asking for their co-operation in seeing that nothing essential is wasted. They listen to him on the air. They write letters to him, explaining about this, grumbling about that, and he makes himself acquainted with the gist of these letters and acts accordingly. That, in my opinion, is the way to run a public department, not just in wartime but at any time. It was a bold but sensible stroke to appoint this economist-turned-big-business-man, without any political experience whatever, the chief of one of our most important ministries, and there is no doubt that it has worked.

I have confidence in the food situation here, though of course large-scale continuous bombing of our ports and a vast new submarine campaign would put our arrangements to a very severe test. But if the Nazis are now more fortunately placed than they were before to try to blockade us, it must be remembered that the amount of shipping now at our disposal is immense, never greater, and that the losses during the last few months have been negligible when compared with the losses in the last war. Nor do I see how Hitler is going to break our own blockade of all his groaning dominions. Our blockade tightens all the time, and if he cannot break it soon, then he will have to march again in search of more quick booty, set another part of Europe ablaze, add a few more millions to his miserable victims, all of whom found their larders stripped bare to feed the insatiable Nazi hosts, who go swarming like giant ants and contributing about as much to civilisation and human happiness as ants would do. But even to call them ants is really falling into the common mistake of flattering their proficiency, for it supposes that there is something mysteriously successful about all they do, whereas the cold truth is that, like all the Germans before them, they are good organisers, and to that they add a complete ruthlessness and also, perhaps more important still, a superb cunning, a racketeer's cunning, in knowing just where the soft and rotten places are in the opposition. To imagine they are any better than this is only to offer them still another soft and rotten place to attack, and already they have had more than their share.

VII. British Reaction to the French Surrender

June 24, 1940

THE PUBLIC reaction here to the humiliating surrender of the Bordeaux Government has been very calm. In fact, there has been a certain feeling of relief. This has been justified by what we have learnt, often in great and convincing detail, from our soldiers, airmen, journalists and others who have now returned from France. Nobody doubts, even yet, the courage of the individual French soldier or the sound qualities of the ordinary French people. We recognise in them still our allies, our friends. They have not been beaten, they have been sold out. Last year, several months before the war began, I remember a lunch at which I sat next to one of the best-known and best-informed French political journalists, who told me that the weak spot in the anti-Nazi front then being hastily formed was France, not because the French people had anything but detestation of the Nazis but because years of political corruption had done their foul work and it might be too late to cure the rot.

That the German army delivered blows of extraordinary force and speed is so obvious that the fact needs no stressing. What, however, does need stressing—and I propose to go on stressing it until I am forcibly silenced—is that those blows were delivered against an opponent who had already been weakened—*from within*. That is the Nazi technique. This cannot be repeated too often. Goering and his bombers, Keitel and his tanks only finished off the work that Ribbentrop, Goebbels and Himmler began years before. These people did well to adopt as their emblem the double cross. The strength of the Nazis does not lie in their armaments, formidable though these may be. It comes from the curiously mixed, bewildering attack, from a technique based on what we might reasonably call years of gangster experience. Other powers, with the possible exception of Russia, still work in separate departments—the foreign offices, the secret services, the armed forces—all more or less going their own way. But the Nazis combine all these—even their economics are part of the aggressive drive—and if the warrior ants are making a frontal attack, you may be sure that the white ants and termites are busy eating out and corrupting the core.

Just imagine, for a moment, that the Germans are lumber jacks and their neighbouring powers are trees. Is the axe that Hitler uses so much stronger and sharper than the one that Ludendorff used in the last war? A great many people assume that it is, just because it appears to send so many apparently stalwart trees crashing down so quickly. But I say, No. I believe that Ludendorff wielded a better axe than Hitler can find. The point is, that these trees that come crashing down after a few hard strokes are not sound timber all the way through, but have been eaten out and hollowed and made rotten inside by years of corruption, which corruption—please note—is itself part of the Nazi attack. In the last war, bridges that were ready to be blown up at a moment's notice were not mysteriously overlooked. Armies did not receive strange conflicting orders. Fighting statesmen who had the confidence of the people were not suddenly removed from authority. You may say that all this is but another proof of the rottenness of the world. That I don't deny. But what I must point out is that the Nazis are masters of the art of increasing that rottenness and taking full advantage of it. They can spot the weak places and don't hesitate to pour poison into them. It is this technique, far more than the weight and speed of their military machine, that makes them so dangerous, the most dangerous enemies that our civilisation has known for a thousand years.

They are very fond of describing themselves—as are the Fascists too—as young virile people, who possess far more of the masculine virtues than the decadent worn-out citizens of the democracies. A great deal of their propaganda, especially in its artful use of films and photographs showing masses of bronzed and stalwart young Nordics, is devoted to creating this picture of themselves. These magnificent young brutes, it is suggested, are irresistible, and soon they will own the earth, for they belong to a new conquering race of super-men. All this is a lot of clever humbug, designed to impress terrified simpletons. Hitler, Goering, Goebbels, Ribbentrop, Himmler—are these the representatives of a young virile race of conquerors? Take a look at them, just listen to their barking and screaming, watch closely all their antics, then judge for yourself. I am well aware of the fact that in this war of machines it is dangerous to overstress the human element, but now I am answering a familiar argument based on the human element, so I ask you to examine all the records so far in this war and find one proof that the Nazi human element is superior to that of the Allies. Time after time, at sea, in the air, on land, whenever the human factor has had full play, these young virile conquerors have shown themselves inferior *as men* to our own so-called decadent worn-out types. This is not only true of the fighting services, it is also true of the civilian population behind them. Winston Churchill stands up, like a man, and openly and honestly tells *his* people that the road before them may be long and hard, offers them "toil and sweat and blood" before victory comes. Does Hitler stand up and talk like that? No. He assures his people over and over again that they are on to a soft thing, and just round the corner is complete victory, when they will be able to swagger over and bully everybody. Why does he have to feed them this stuff? Simply because his young virile all-conquering people haven't the stomach for the hard truth. They have to exist in a kind of opium dream of conquest and grandeur, otherwise they're going to lose heart, their young virile all-conquering hearts.

[45]

The quality of their human material, either military or civilian, is not a source of strength but of weakness to the Nazis, and they know it. For this reason they don't even use their toughest men in the front line. They use them as storm troopers to bully and cow the poor wretches at the back. Nobody in his senses is going to deny the sheer quantity and weight of German armaments. We may be lost, and civilisation lost with us, unless we can reply with plane for plane, tank for tank, gun for gun. That is why we don't hesitate to ask, not for men, but for every possible kind of defensive and offensive weapon—planes, machine-guns, rifles—anything that helps to make these madmen appreciate the only argument they understand.

Even more than the sheer weight of armaments the main strength of the Nazis lies in their absolutely unscrupulous and diabolically cunning technique of attack from within accompanying the attack from without. They have yet to meet—though I believe they are going to meet it now—a really tough unbroken opposition, a people who are in one resolute mind about opposing them to the death, a tree that has not been hollowed out and made rotten inside so that it will come down after a few sharp blows of the axe. All the whispers of defeatism, all those murmurs of "Oh, we can't do any good now, it's too late," are part of this long insidious attack from within. For years the Nazis have known that when the hour struck, there could not be such a thing as genuine neutrality, they knew that "Who is not with us, is against us," and they laid their plans accordingly. Day and night, ceaselessly, during those years, they have felt for the rotten spots in every corner of the world, and the very tolerance and good-humour of the democracies provided them with superb opportunities, of which they took instant advantage. For these are men who have shed all illusions but one—a belief in their own ultimate greatness. If you can keep in mind always their gangster back-ground, then you have always a clue to their mentality and their methods. Remember too that they have discovered that sheer impudence pays, so that nothing is too impudent for them. They feel they can't overestimate the stupidity of the world.

A striking example of this impudence has been the broadcasting of the ceremony of signing this miserable armistice in France. The German radio accounts of it for listeners outside Germany was all solemn, fake chivalry, full of apparent sympathy for the noble vanquished opponent. But the radio account for German listeners was full of savage glee, venom, vindictiveness and hate, like the terms of the armistice itself, which are about as honourable as such familiar German devices as raising the white flag and then firing. Those terms don't surprise anybody here. We seem to know the Nazis better than Marshal Pétain does, with his pathetic "one soldier to another" plea. And we wait to see what can be saved

out of the wreck. The people here are grand, and my
only complaint is that now they need to be handled
rather more imaginatively, with more of an honest-man-
to-man spirit and with less of the pussy-footing manner,
with which we are all becoming rather impatient.

VIII. The Intellectual and the Battle Against the Nazis

June 26, 1940

I WANT to consider the relation between the intellectual and this battle against the Nazis. By the "intellectual" I mean the writer, the artist, the scientist, the scholar, the teacher or the student, although of course any listener who cares for the things of the mind and the spirit is at liberty to enroll himself or herself as an "intellectual."

This topic suggests itself because from American reports and periodicals I have gathered that there is a considerable and very noisy movement in some American universities and colleges in favour of pacifism and what can only be called defeatism. In other words, a great many well-meaning young Americans are busy saying just what Goebbels and his gang want them to say. I know very well that these young people have not the least desire to help the Nazis. Nevertheless, they *are* helping the Nazis. They are even taking advantage of America's magnificently democratic educational system to further a cause—Nazism—that is notorious for having destroyed the educational system and indeed all the real cultural life of its country, and is now busy destroying the education and culture of its neighbours. For example, for generations now American students, writers, artists have looked to France—to that great treasure city of free enquiry, artistic experiment, and wit, Paris—for guidance and inspiration. They can look no longer. The France they loved is now in bondage. Paris—that bright citadel of learning, culture, wit—is now in the grip of men, who having no learning, culture or wit themselves, hate all others who possess these resources of the mind and spirit, men who have the outlook of police spies and brutal sergeants, men who live in a mental darkness themselves and are determined that everybody else should live in the same darkness, a huge gang that no matter what power it may control remains today what it always was—namely, riff-raff. No man or woman who has the least claims to intellect can be ignorant of what we all owe to the exquisitely clear, brave, witty spirit of France. But what do we owe to these Nazis? What has come so far from that huge armed camp of theirs? Not one beautiful thing, not one wise sentence, not one glimmer of light. Nothing but offers of bribes, boasts, threats, tanks and bombers. Moreover, the Nazis always deliberately make the complete destruction of the intellectual life one of their very first tasks.

For example, in Poland, it was the intellectuals who were immediately pounced upon and obliterated. Universities were invaded by gangs of storm troopers and Gestapo officials. Elderly professors, including men of the very highest distinction in their own valuable fields of learning, men with world-wide reputations, were thrown into concentration camps, beaten, bullied, tortured, murdered. The facts are there for anybody to read. Everything possible—and many things that most of us thought impossible in this century—was done to destroy the intellectual and cultural life of this unhappy country, and I have no doubt whatever that a similar obliteration is taking place—or will shortly take place—in Norway, Holland, Belgium and the occupied territories of France. The Nazis may come to some kind of sullen terms with the peasants and the workers, whose assistance they need, but from the moment of their entry into any country the intellectuals are doomed. That is why I don't hesitate to say that if there ever was, in the whole history of this world, a conflict that was fought for the benefit of the intellectual it is this present battle against the Nazi. For some kinds of men and women, there may be the shadow of an excuse to stand aside, but for the intellectual, no matter whether he lives in London, New York, Toronto, San Francisco, or in Patagonia, there is not the tiniest shadow of an excuse. If he stands aside, he must realise that he is merely sheltering behind the backs of other men and women, that the very meetings at which he sneers at the British Empire can only be held now because there still exists, as the first shield between him and these Nazi hordes, the unbroken might of that Empire. If a man wants to say "Nobody's attacked me yet, so I'm not worrying—let somebody else do the worrying," he has a perfect right to say so, and it's not for me to dictate his attitude, but what he cannot

[51]

do is to claim for this short-sighted and ungallant escapism a high moral tone, a "holier-than-thou" point of view, because it simply won't do.

There are some English authors who are now across the water, no doubt writing their books and film scripts under conditions no longer possible to us on this side. That's all right—if they can do it—so long as they realise that what enables them still to write in comparative security is the fact that simple young men, not very brilliant, not very wise, but devoted to their duty and brave as lions, are manning the planes of the Royal Air Force and the ships of the Royal Navy. And though my own literary work has of necessity come to a temporary standstill, and though we are now faced with agonising decisions about our families, I tell you frankly that I don't envy these former colleagues of mine who are on the other side of the water, because I believe that our state of mind is better than theirs. If we win through, then after years of indecision and bickering and doubt and fear and heart-burning, we shall have accomplished something positive and great, and can go forward to make the world anew, fit for its thinkers, scientists, artists.

If we go down—and we shall go down fighting, as the ships of the Navy have always gone down fighting, blazing away until the waters closed over them—then the lights will be going out all over the globe, and they are welcome to the darkness that will be left.

You remember the story of Nelson at the battle of Copenhagen. A shot through the mainmast knocked the splinters about; and he observed to one of his officers with a smile, "It is warm work, and this may be the last to any of us at any moment." And then he added, with emotion, "But mark you—I would not be elsewhere for thousands." Well, we can't all be Nelsons, but there are a lot of his kinsmen still living in this island. And one reason why I wouldn't be elsewhere for thousands is because of the people here, the ordinary common folk. They're wonderful. And every time Goebbels and his gang cry "Bogey-bogey!" their courage and their spirits rise higher still.

Even those few intellectuals here who tried to pretend this conflict was none of their business have now completely turned round, as one of them, the editor of our new highbrow magazine, *Horizon,* freely confesses in his editorial this month. To give these young men their due, they may write and talk a good deal of pretentious and precious stuff at times, and make a policy of not approving of or joining in things just because other people do approve of or join in them, but they don't propose to be rattled and panicked by the Goebbels bogey-bogey machine. And, mind you, every effort has been made by the Nazis to take advantage of the sheer terror of modern warfare that has lodged itself in so many subconscious minds. They've done everything possible to paralyse opposition by first invading the subconscious and the imagination of more sensitive minds, suggesting a dark host of fears and terrors, creating a smoke-screen of defeatism.

But fortunately the British are not a very impressionable people. The ordinary folk are probably the hardest to rattle and panic of any in the world. This is partly due to the fact that they are not very imaginative and always incline to be free-and-easy and complacent. As raw material for the diabolical art of Goebbels, who is used to dealing with a rather neurotic people, our folk are quite hopeless. If they haven't broken his heart yet, they surely will. But there is another and deeper reason why our people are rising and not descending in spirit, and this may be difficult for some intellectuals to understand. The English, as several foreign philosophers and observers have pointed out more than once, are at heart a very religious people. I don't mean by that they have a passion of religious observances and ritual, because they haven't, but they have a profound faith in the moral order of the universe. As a man put it in a letter to me that I opened this morning: "The position," he writes, "is not so much that God is on our side but that we are on God's side." There is a faith in our people everywhere that, in spite of our many mistakes and our numerous imperfections, we are fighting so that the good life shall continue in this world, for we also know that what we are fighting—this Nazi doctrine that nothing matters but force and fraud—must be the enemy of the good life. And for people who feel this deeply, as millions do here, there are invisible sources of help and power, great unseen stocks of courage and initiative.

IX. What Chances of an Invasion?

June 28, 1940

THE RAIDS we've had this week—not yet on the blitzkrieg scale but for all that fairly big raids, some of them—must be giving the German Air Staff a bigger headache than they've given us, because, unless they've been trying out a lot of new pilots and observers, they have been a failure. To begin with, they haven't done much damage, to military objectives or to anything else. Some civilians have been killed and wounded, though far less than are killed and wounded by road accidents in the same number of days, and against that must be set the fact that the Germans have lost, by death or capture, the services of a number of trained men, whose services they can ill afford to lose. Again, the effect of these raids on morale here has been to raise it and not lower it. The ordinary people seem to be much livelier than they were last winter, when they found it—as indeed I did—all rather boring. Now they're full of beans, and also enjoying the presence everywhere of soldiers. London streets are filled with Dominion troops, seeing the sights—big, tough guys most of them, and spoiling for a fight. I'm told that the very rich are a bit gloomy, but the few times I've come in contact with the very rich, they always seemed gloomy; and I think the kindest thing to do with the very rich is to stop them from being very rich, which we're now doing good and hard. The typical Whitehall officials are not exactly full of fun and gusto, but that's not because they're afraid of anything but because they're Whitehall officials and superior persons, and feel they have to behave like mandarins. But the people, on whom I pin my faith, are all right.

So is Mr. George Bernard Shaw, with whom I lunched today. He looked more robust and twinkling than I've seen him look these last two or three years, and never stopped talking. He said he'd always advised the world never to rouse the English because once they were aroused they were capable of more heroisms and atrocities than anybody else. He also said that the way to settle the Irish difficulty was to start a cry in Eire that the awful English were not giving that protection to Eire that they were giving to the other members of the Commonwealth, that the English were denying poor ould Ireland her airplanes, battleships and tanks, that it was just another big grievance, and—faith!—they'll be holding meetings demanding that the British forces be sent over.

I've never seen Bernard Shaw in better spirits, and here he is in London, waiting, like the rest of us, for the next chapter of the blitzkrieg. We're promised it next week, and news comes from Zurich this morning that Hitler is planning a triumphal entry into Berlin on August the first after victory over Britain. Orders have already been given for the erection of stands for this victory parade in Berlin. The publication of this stuff has a triple purpose: to hearten the Germans, who apparently must need it very badly, in spite of their victories; to impress the neutrals; and to try and panic the people of this island, who are a kind of people that Goebbels simply doesn't understand.

It's worth noticing that in case this programme miscarries, the Nazis are already preparing their big propaganda for the period *after* this blitzkrieg has failed. The object of this will be to persuade all the people in the countries conquered by Germany that they will go hungry simply because the wicked British are blockading the continent. The real truth being that they will go hungry because the Nazis are now busy stealing all the produce of these countries in order to feed the Nazi armies and munition workers. And no matter how much food you or ourselves or anybody else pours into these countries, it will still be taken by the Nazis to feed their armies.

There's a very good cartoon in tonight's *Evening Standard* by my friend David Low—one of the best cartoonists in the world—and in it we see a ragged woman, France, and five ragged children, Belgium, Poland, Holland, Norway, Denmark, who have a large placard round their necks. Behind them is the immense figure of Goering, who has a sack over one shoulder and a pig in one hand, while the other hand grasps the shaft of a cart that is piled high with sacks and boxes labelled 'Looted Food.' Goering is saying to these ragged and wistful figures, "I gave you a nice placard in exchange, didn't I?" And this placard that he gave them, to hang round their necks, says, "Appeal to kind hearts in U.S.A. Please send food to the women and children of starving Europe and help to beat the wicked British blockade."

Please remember that it was this Goering, and not any English politician, who used to cry "Guns before butter." Well, this wicked blockade trick is the next on the list for the German propaganda machine if the blitzkrieg against us fails to land Hitler on his triumphant entry into Berlin on August the first.

What are the chances of this blitzkrieg against us? I've been collecting cautious official opinion about invasion. In the first place, it's possible, of course, that the German General Staff have in hand methods as surprising to us as the methods in Flanders and France were to them. It's possible, but it's not likely. I suspect most of the surprises have already been sprung—though no doubt they've one or two new tricks up their sleeves. And it's very important to remember that the methods in Flanders and France depended upon a good deal of fifth-column cooperation, on a lot of successful undercover work in advance. How many times during that campaign, from the first invasion of Holland to the armistice in France, did it happen that something of the highest military importance—such as the blowing of a bridge already mined—was somehow forgotten to be put into operation against the Germans? I was reading only this morning about a certain Monsieur Amouralle, who was no less a person than the secretary to the French Senate and was sentenced to death by the Reynaud government for having conveyed much valuable information to German agents. And somehow the sentence was not carried out. I can't believe that sort of thing is going to happen on any scale in this island. Whatever happens, it's going to be a fight, and not half a fight, and half a sell-out.

But apart from this fifth-column danger, we've learnt a lot from what happened in the Low Countries and France. There aren't going to be a number of nice aerodromes left for them to land on—or any other large open spaces—or any convenient supplies of petrol to loot. And now that all our aircraft are back from France, this place is bristling with fighting planes, and large slow troop-carrying planes will have an awfully bad time against our hurricanes and spitfires. They may attempt to gain complete superiority in the air over one area, for purposes of large-scale invasion, but they tried and failed to do this at Dunkirk, where we couldn't have carried out the evacuation unless we'd thoroughly established local superiority. Our whole system of aerial reconnaissance, observer corps work, searchlight and anti-aircraft battery defences, plus the fighters, is now very formidable, easily the best in the world, with an amazingly intricate network of communications between all these various defences, and the cost of large-scale penetration of these defences is going to be terrific to the Germans in both machines and men. In Flanders and France our air force worked under grave disadvantages, because they were continually compelled to move back their aerodromes, but here at home, working under familiar and friendly conditions, with every facility for repairs and so on, they are at an immense advantage. If the German pilots didn't enjoy meeting the R.A.F. in France, they're certainly not going to have a happy time with them over England.

So much for the air. Now for the sea. Here we must make an important distinction between invading and raiding. Nobody doubts that it is possible for the Germans to raid the shores of this country, perhaps landing several thousands of men. We have an enormous coast-line, a great many possible landing places, so that in spite of all our defences, a few thousand can set foot on these shores. But then what? We have more than a million and a quarter men under arms, and they are being rapidly trained to meet the specific problems of attempted invasion. These raiders can make a great nuisance of themselves, but their chances of either getting very far into Britain or of ever seeing their Fatherland again are very small. Invasion proper, as distinct from raiding, needs a considerable army, with all the necessary massive equipment, and an absolute armada of transport vessels. Please remember that even with full command of the sea it took weeks and weeks at the beginning of the war to transport the B.E.F. across the Channel to France, without any hindrance of any kind.

It is more than likely that if this large-scale invasion is tried, it will be attempted across the narrowest part of the Channel with an immense fleet of motor torpedo boats and flat-bottom boats towed by tugs, and there'll have to be a whale of a lot of them. Now these boats can only operate successfully in calm water, and there are not many days in the year when the Channel is calm. That was our great stroke of luck at the evacuation of Dunkirk, which wouldn't have been possible at all in rough weather. Landing an army is a very tricky job even when you have complete command of the sea, as our own naval men can tell you. When you haven't complete command of the sea, when at any moment a few destroyers may be let loose among your huge flotillas of tugs and crowded flat-bottom boats, when the wind may blow hard at any moment too and the hungry seas rise with it, when you are expected at the other side by batteries of artillery and strongly entrenched infantry, bristling with machine guns, the prospect is not hopeful for the invader.

But, you may say, the invader may ignore the expected places, the narrow Channel, and try elsewhere, across the wider stretches of the Channel or even across the North Sea. But then he has to meet further difficulties. The voyage is too long to be undertaken during the hours of darkness, and an armada in full daylight is a perfect target. Moreover, for this longer voyage, across rough seas, he must use much larger vessels, and these vessels not only present our warships with better targets but also will soon find themselves in difficulties among our mine fields. But even supposing this fleet of large transport vessels successfully eludes both the navy and the mine fields, it has still to find some kind of harbour, and there is no undefended harbour of any size in this island. Then again, even if this first fleet of transports by a series of lucky chances arrives here and lands its men, that is only the beginning of invasion, for the invader must keep his forces regularly supplied with food and munitions, he must keep that fleet sailing regularly backwards and forwards to this island, and what chance has he of doing that? Nobody knows better than the authorities in this country all the difficulties, dangers and expense of maintaining an expeditionary force overseas, and the fact that for once we are freed from that necessity makes our position just now, with troops, ships, supplies, immensely strong. We are relatively much stronger, in spite of all these recent disasters to our allies, than we were in the last war, and I still believe that Hitler's Germany, for all its blitzkriegs and triumphant marches, is not as strong as the Kaiser's Germany was. Where it is strongest is where the older Germany was weakest, and that is—in its propaganda machine.

X. Nazi Propaganda for Export

July 1, 1940

YESTERDAY I talked with a very intelligent young diplomat who has just joined one of the neutral legations here in London. I asked him what struck him particularly about the people in England. He said that two things struck him. First, after the depression and fear and panic of Europe, he was struck by the calm, the cheerfulness, the resolution of the people here. There was, he felt, some deep intangible element here that Hitler and the Nazis couldn't understand, for it was altogether outside their experience. The second thing that struck him was this—that whereas in Europe people everywhere hated the Nazis, it was a personal hatred, and a lot of them wouldn't mind having some Nazis of their own—but that here in England what the people hated was the wicked philosophy—if you can call it a philosophy—the evil values of the Nazis, rather than the Nazis themselves. Here, in short, it wasn't a personal hatred but a moral detestation that fired the people's resistance.

Now this is true. A familiar old jibe at Britain is that whenever she wants to do something purely for her own interest, she contrives to make a moral issue out of it and so give the impression that she is not acting from self-interest but from altruism. This is called a typical example of British hypocrisy. But people who talk like this simply don't understand the British character—or rather, the nature of the ordinary British people. The fact is, you can't rouse the British—and I suspect that this is true too of the American people—*except* by making a moral issue out of any question. We may at times be led by cynics, but they have to hide their cynicism when they are calling up the people to move. I made this very point, months before this war broke out, in my book *Rain Upon Godshill*, where I said: "There still exists in us a deep vein of moral idealism. Cruel things may have been done in the name of the British Empire, but those things have always been hastily hidden away from the sight of the British people, for fear of their sudden anger. And the people as a whole will not move and march unless the cause is given some cover and show of nobility, which is what the foreign observer, aghast at such hypocrisy, hardly ever understands. In 1914 Asquith and Grey may not have been crusading for 'gallant little Belgium'; but the people were, for I was one of them myself and I know. We share this strain of thoughtless but genuine moral idealism, of course, with the Americans. . . ."

That's what I wrote before the war, and everything that has happened since bears me out. The British people are sustained now by a deep moral—you might almost say *religious*—detestation of the whole Nazi way of life, and they will never make any truce with it. You have to get down to this to see the issue clearly. On any other more superficial level than the moral-religious level everything is immensely complicated because our conflicts now, in this disintegrating world, cannot be understood on simple nationalist political-economic lines. The Nazis realise this better than our Government does—as Sir Norman Angell points out in a letter to the *News Chronicle* this morning, where he proposes that we should stop handling our problems as if they were merely nationalistic ones, as they were in the last war, and see this as a final conflict between a projected Nazi-Fascist world and a world in which a liberal civilisation is still possible.

The Nazis take full advantage of this present complication and confusion, and see to it that their propaganda is going in several—and often contradictory—directions at once. In Germany the Nazis are nationalists pure and simple, if it's possible to apply the words "pure" and "simple" to such people in any connection. That is, they tell their people they are fighting simply for the glory and aggrandisement of Germany. The Germans, they announce, are the superior people, the master race, and sooner or later all other nations will have to bow down before them and work for these Nordic conquerors. That is the line at home—good old nationalism with a dose or two of rubbishy race theory and bogus mysticism. But this stuff is not exported, because they know it won't export. Nobody outside Germany wants to be told that he should help the Nazis because the Germans are a master race. It never occurs to anybody outside Germany

[65]

that the Germans are a master race. In fact, nobody out-side Germany admires or likes these Nazi Germans at all. So for outside propaganda, there has to be quite a different line of selling talk.

It takes two forms, which really contradict each other. One is the attack upon what are called the "pluto-democracies"—Britain and the United States. The idea is that the Germans and Italians are poor hard-working folk denied their share of the good things of life by the rich democracies. The Nazi has arrived to redress this balance. He is, in this picture of himself, the revolu-tionary, who is going to rescue everybody from the clutches of mysterious Jewish capitalists. The fact that neither Britain nor the United States *is* dominated by Jewish capitalists does not worry the Nazis at all, because they know that they have only to keep on repeating a thumping great lie for some idiots to believe it. Hitler tells these idiots that quite plainly in his book, which creates a very paradoxical situation because if you be-lieve what he writes, then obviously you must not believe what he says, and if you believe what he says, then you must not believe what he writes—so where are you? A typical example of this series of new German fairy tales is that the English press is entirely controlled and owned by Jewish financiers. When you point out that in fact it isn't, they'll tell you that you don't know a Jewish financier when you see one. Probably by this time I'm referred to in Nazi propaganda circles as "the well-known Jewish author."

Well, that's one line—the revolutionary rescuing-Europe-from-the-rich method of attack. The opposite line, which is quite contradictory, is made less fuss about in public but a great deal more in private, when the Nazis are persuading the rich reactionaries, as they did in France, to come into their camp. Here, they represent themselves as the opponents of revolution, the strong men who can protect the rich right-wingers and their investments against the revolt of their own people. Undoubtedly they made great play with this in France, where the reactionaries, to their eternal shame, preferred Hitler to their own angry people. And it is in this secret anti-revolutionary propaganda that the Nazis are most dangerous. They go round muttering the same old story about being the bulwark against Communism, and that very soon, when Western Europe has been cleaned up and thoroughly policed, they will turn against Russia. This is what a few rich fools, in several different countries, have swallowed, forgetting what happened in Germany to the steel magnates who first contributed their millions to the Nazi chest.

So there you have it. The Nazis are nationalists at home, and anti-nationalists—both revolutionaries and counter-revolutionaries, just as you prefer it—in their propaganda abroad. From the first, long before they were heard of outside Germany, they have worked the trick of being all things to all men. We have all wasted far too much time trying to discover the political and economic programme and philosophy of Nazism. It has

no such programme and philosophy. It is purely oppor-
tunist and irrational. It represents a drive for power, on
the part of a small group of bad men, headed by a
megalomaniac, at all costs. Its basis is psychological.

A young German lawyer, Sebastian Haffner, has just
brought out a book called *Germany: Jekyll or Hyde*,
and he makes these points very clear. "Hitler," he says,
"serves no idea, no nation, no statesmanlike conception,
but exclusively the propulsion of his ego. . . . His
aims . . . are: first, maintenance and extension of his
personal power; secondly, revenge on all groups of persons and institutions against whom he feels resentment,
and they are many; thirdly, the staging of scenes out of
Wagner's operas with Adolf Hitler as chief protagonist.
All else is pretence and tactic." I advise everyone to read
this book by Sebastian Haffner. It is a penetrating
analysis and a brilliant performance.

And now we come to what puzzles so many good folk.
How have these Nazis, with their lies, deceit, vindictiveness and cruelty, succeeded in finding admirers and
followers outside Germany, in establishing those now-
famous fifth columns that undoubtedly exist everywhere? The answer is twofold. First they have spent
more time, trouble and money on propaganda and
espionage than any people in the history of the world.
They have made political corruption a fine and flourish-
ing art. Secondly, they realised that their own psychological types exist everywhere, even though not in the
same degree as they exist in Germany. The restless, dis-

satisfied youth who finds he cannot fit in anywhere in
the existing scheme, who wants a swaggering and exciting life, dashing about in fast cars and beating people up,
is fine raw material for Nazi and Fascist doctrines. The
unsuccessful and inefficient little professional man or
shopkeeper who attributes all his lack of success to the
unfair competition of the Jews or something of that sort,
is also ready to lend an ear to those Nazi fairy tales.
Then, much more dangerous than those other two, are
the men who are very ambitious, unscrupulous, cleverish
and unfortunately have no particular talent, except a
minor talent for intrigue and cheap mob oratory. They
are men who are always disturbed by a gnawing vanity
and a sense of grievance because their great but mysterious abilities have not been fully recognised. And they
have usually not been trusted by existing political
parties. There is something about them—often a shifty
or cruel look in the eye—that makes ordinary decent
people mistrust them. And though they can shout themselves hoarse—denouncing "Jewish capitalists" and "Bol-
shevik agitators" and the rest—actually these men have
no real political convictions; they stand for nothing but
themselves; they have a deep-rooted contempt for most
other persons as well as a sense of their grandeur; and
they hate all the democratic virtues—the free-and-easy
arguments, the give-and-take, the tolerance and humour.
And they recognise in the Nazi leaders their own blood
brothers, master specimens of their own rotten type, and
they see how this upheaval, which is really the corrup-

tion of the world coming to a head, might put power, notoriety, wealth, and many opportunities for personal aggrandisement and revenge, in their way. And there are your Quislings and your Mosleys, wanting to be little Hitlers and Goerings, ready if necessary to betray a few million of their fellow-countrymen into slavery.

Just notice that among these converts you never find men of real distinction, men of great and world-recognised talent, but only men who feel they ought to be famous though for what they hardly know. Even among the Germans, the Einsteins and Thomas Manns are all on the other side, defying and disdaining the Nazis. And here in England this defiance of and deep moral scorn for the Nazis have possessed almost every section of the people, with the small exception of the types I've listed already. I believe these to be as small in influence as they are in numbers. *They have no influence whatever* over the present British Government.

XI. An Answer to the Doubts of American Commentators

July 3, 1940

I HAVE NEVER pretended to be the victim of the artistic temperament, whatever that means, but I have my moods the same as the next man, and at the moment I am in the mood for some plain, blunt speaking.

I've been collecting what seem to be the chief criticisms and doubts of those American commentators who think no help should be given to our side, and I'll try to answer them one by one as clearly and honestly as I possibly can. First then the fear that the representatives of the former appeasement school still in the Government here might act as Laval and his group did in France. For my part I don't believe this can happen. The whole temper of the country is against it. This is to assume—and I don't assume it—that the supporters of Munich would favour a compromise peace now. A small number might, but their leaders wouldn't. But why, you ask, are these Munich men still in office? The plain answer is because they happen to represent the political party that still has a large majority in the House of Commons, and it's impossible to have a General Election with a blitzkrieg round the corner. Nevertheless, in spite of this Parliamentary majority the real power resides in Mr. Winston Churchill and the labour

[71]

group, who between them, command the full confidence of the country. Government policy here on all really big issues must rest on public confidence. If the public, supported by the Press, withdraws that confidence the Government is sunk. Another thing, the greater the crisis here, the greater the power of Mr. Churchill on the one hand and of the labour group, on the other hand. All the fighting services, all organised labour and the great body of public opinion will respect and honour their decisions. The situation in France was entirely different.

Next, doubt that though we may all talk big about fighting on and on, this is because we don't really know what a blitzkrieg means, and that when we go through what Belgium and France went through we may soon change our tune. There are many different possible replies to this and some of them dealing with the internal conditions of Belgium and France would take too long to make here. I will in fact content myself with one reply—namely, that we have a great many people here who do know what a blitzkrieg really means, and know it better than any American journalists, and these people are the various members of our fighting services who came back from Belgium and France. There isn't much about that blitzkrieg over there that these fellows don't know, and some of the stories they tell of how the Germans succeeded often, not by force, but by sheer impudence, are very revealing, and I have yet to meet one of them, Army, Air Force, Navy, who isn't cheerfully confident they're all absolutely on their toes. Of course we can't tell what we may be called upon to go through, and it would be stupid to pretend it all looks being fun and games, but we simply refuse to begin knocking at the knees because the German propaganda machine is now screaming blitzkrieg at us. Nor do some of us see why people who speak the same language as ourselves and share the same political ideals should lend Herr Hitler their assistance by joining these screamers. Don't forget that this screaming in advance, these panic tactics, are half the game. Once you've got people rattled and on the run you don't even need a real seventy-ton tank to chase them about, for any tin thing that runs and makes a noise will do.

And I must add this, that the more I learn about the French campaign, the more respect I have for the Nazi propaganda and espionage departments, and the less I have for their army. I don't mean by that it's a bad army. Its organisation and drive are obviously superb, but what its real honest-to-God fighting qualities are we don't know, because those qualities have not yet been fully tested. They've not been tested to anything like the same degree that ours have, for our men, fantastically out-numbered and with Allies on their flanks melting away, have at least fought one magnificent rear-guard action.

Which brings me to the next line of criticism, that we have a trick of interpreting every disaster as if it were actually an advantage. Poland, Norway, Holland

and Belgium, even the collapse of France: these have all been conjured into mysterious gains of ours. Well, if this trick were regarded merely as an excuse for more and more complacency I'd agree with its savagest critics. And there was, I grant you, far too much complacency up to the last two months. This was due to two different causes. First a bad Government policy. Secondly, the unusual slowness of the British public mind in realising that anything genuinely new is happening at all. We are the slowest people in the world to grasp the fact that changes are taking place. But this cuts both ways. The same slowness and tenacity that first make for complacency, afterwards, when that complacency has been thoroughly disturbed, make for a most stubborn determination to hold on at all costs. We may be the most complacent, perhaps the most self-satisfied people in the world, but we are also, I think, easily the least hysterical, the very hardest to panic, and nobody who has read or heard the Prime Minister's recent speeches or the speeches of any members of his Cabinet or the pronouncements of our press, can pretend that we are still being fed with soothing syrup. It is the Germans now, in spite of their victories, who are being treated by their leaders with such honeyed flattery, who are being promised that all their efforts are nearly over, told that they needn't worry any longer. This fact seems to me intensely significant.

A further criticism made by some American newspaper men is that the whole rhythm of our war effort is too slow; that our ruling and official classes still cling too much to peace-time privileges, such as week-ends away from work, and so on; that there is not enough hard drive of leadership. With this criticism I have some sympathy, but then so has the entire press and millions and millions of the public itself. If nobody had noticed these facts but a few newspaper correspondents I should be greatly alarmed, but as it is the whole country, except the more mandarin-like members of these official classes who will simply have to get on or get out, is demanding this fiercer tempo. And what the country demands the country will have if it is not having it already.

This brings us to the story carefully put out by the Nazis and now used as one of the alibis by the Bordeaux Government, that we did not support France as we ought to have done. With this criticism I have no patience whatever. It has Berlin written all over it. We mobilised a Navy that has done everything expected of it. We provided France with an Air Force that the French themselves praised in the very highest terms. The Expeditionary Force we sent was small, though no smaller than the French military authorities had reason to expect, but efficient, and it fulfilled all the demands made upon it. To blame us for the political corruption that ruined the brave French people is monstrous.

We should be foolish to go on under-estimating Germany's striking force, but is it any wiser, isn't it even more dangerous, to over-estimate that force? To believe that it is so powerful and super-efficient that Britain cannot stand up against it, and therefore it is a waste of valuable material to provide us with arms and munitions. It may be that Hitler has a few new and wonderful tricks up his sleeve, though it's as well to remember that he's not the only person with a sleeve, and that the British have always been more inventive than the Germans.

The fact remains that so far Hitler's record against us isn't impressive. In the first few months of the war, the U-boats were going to sink everything we had afloat, but actually they proved far less effective than they were in the last war. Then planes bombing and machine-gunning everything they saw were going to make sea traffic impossible, but they didn't. Then the pocket battleships, which we were told were very difficult propositions because they were more heavily armed than cruisers fast enough to catch them and much faster than the battleships that could out-gun them, were going to raid and capture and sink our ships all over the world, but what in fact have they done? The *Emden* in the last war did more than all these pocket battleships put together. Then Goering said that no British planes would penetrate his defences, whereas the R.A.F. are bombing Germany day and night. The great German Air Force was going to sweep everything before it. I remember coming across an account of the German and Allied Air Forces printed in a very popular American weekly just after the outbreak of war, and according to this singularly ill-informed journalist not only was

still full of devilment. And that's the kind of man we want for this hour, not weary old muddlers, mumbling platitudes and secretly terrified of the situation in which they find themselves.

Mr. Churchill began his speech slowly and solemnly, as well he might, for the disastrous straits of the Bordeaux Government put the British Cabinet in a terrible position, in which they were compelled to take—as he said—"grim and sombre decisions." One foul circumstance, in all this welter of weakness, he did not mention, and that was the widespread feeling among the French naval officers and men that the Nazis would take action, if necessary, against their families. This is the way the new Germany does things, these are the tactics of these Siegfrieds of the Swastika—they strike at you through your women and children. Can you imagine Britain or the United States or any power with the least pretence of being civilised resorting to foul racketeer methods of this kind? What is the use of these people turning on their streams of propaganda, day and night, when every action they do contradicts every one of their pretensions. It is not only that they have extinguished the last glimmer of that chivalry and sense of masculine honour which marks the difference between warfare, even now, and mere mass murder; but they make no pretence, in their actions as distinguished from their talk, of even behaving with elementary decency. Mr. Churchill might well be slow and solemn, for he, like all of us, still respects and loves France herself; and he took care, as we all must do, to make a careful distinction between the Bordeaux Government and the French people themselves. But as he went on, in his own masterly style, to describe the series of actions forced upon our Cabinet, who were absolutely unanimous in their agreement as to the necessity of such action, Mr. Churchill became more animated, altogether warmer and more dramatic in tone. His references to the obedience of the Bordeaux Government to their new German masters had a fine edge of scorn. As he went on with his tale of naval operations—the boarding of the French ships here, the ultimatums at Alexandria, the fair alternatives offered to the ships at Oran, the battle at Oran, only undertaken by our squadron after every possible alternative we had offered had been refused—you could feel a certain gusto coming into and warming and heightening his tone.

This man, you knew, loved the ships and sailormen with whom he had worked for so long, during two wars, at the Admiralty. This was, you felt, his element, just as it is most certainly not Herr Hitler's element as very shortly he may discover. On the other hand, although there was an instinctive delight in rapid and decisive action to be perceived in Mr. Churchill's tone, there was not the very least suggestion of any vindictive glee at the terrible reply we had been compelled to make to the Bordeaux Government. The French officers and men, who had been thus forced to turn their guns upon their old comrades, had, he told us, fought bravely and well. He did not add, although one felt the thought was there, the irony and pity of the fact that many of these guns, in action perhaps for the first time, were now firing for a rotten cause, as the result of defeatism and treachery and a distrust—which is fatal for any democracy—a distrust, I say, of the French people on the part of some of their own politicians and leaders.

No doubt the Nazi propagandists will make capital out of this strangest naval battle in all modern history. But the two lessons to be learnt from it, to my mind, are these: First, don't rat on the people, which is what the Bordeaux Government have done from first to last. Secondly, don't imagine that the British can't act suddenly and decisively when the moment comes. We may be slow before the issue seems clear to us, but once it is clear, we can strike at once and can strike hard. And anybody who heard Mr. Churchill this afternoon would have felt at once that he was a man of this metal and calibre. He could strike, would strike, and go on hitting. This was his final topic, after he had told us that the bulk of the French Fleet was now either in our hands or so badly crippled that it will be useless to the enemy, to the Germans, who have only a shadow of a fleet, to the Italians, who if they had come out and had a fight might have done us a sad mischief but thought it more prudent to stay at home. Yes, his final topic was an indignant and forceful repudiation of the idea that he and his fellow ministers were for one moment contemplating any compromise with the Nazis.

Today is Independence Day. It is a good day to

realise all over again that now we mean what we say just as Americans meant what they said nearly a hundred and seventy years ago. Our aim is the independence of Europe—and indeed of the whole world—from this nightmare of Nazi threats, murderous invasion, and slavery. And I wish everyone could have seen and heard the House of Commons this afternoon, when its Prime Minister concluded, in ringing tones, his implacable challenge to these dictators. They jumped to their feet, every member there, turned to their undaunted leader, and cheered and cheered. No one could have failed to feel, as I did, that here is a man worthy of the great cause of human liberty.

XIII. The Fundamental Issue of the War

July 7, 1940

IT'S A GOOD thing, these days, to learn the very latest news, but it's an equally good thing to take stock of the general situation now and then, therefore I propose to examine the whole problem of this world-wide conflict and to try and decide exactly for what we here are fighting.

Now I spent the first two or three months of this war travelling up and down the country, for the Press, looking at camps, aerodromes, naval bases, munition and aircraft factories and the like, and during these many weeks of travel I talked with thousands of people belonging to every walk of life, and especially with young army and naval and air-force officers and men and the younger men in the factories. Two things struck me. First, the whole atmosphere was entirely different from that of the last war, which began almost as if it were part of some hysterical summer holiday, with a great deal of singing and shouting and flag-waving and rioting against foreigners and belligerent high jinks in the old-fashioned wartime manner. This war opened very soberly, with none of that noise and hysteria. The ordinary people were united and determined, but if they were not depressed, were not elated either, but were like people faced with an unpleasant but urgently necessary task. The second thing that struck me, after talking to hundreds and hundreds of the younger men, was that all of them were asking themselves—and me— what kind of world would come out of this war. They were all ready to do everything demanded of them, were united in their determination to work and fight— like blazes—against Hitler, but they did want to feel that at the end of it all they wouldn't find themselves back again in the kind of world that began this conflict.

Now here, I think, the Chamberlain Government missed a great opportunity. It is true that on several occasions, notably in some speeches by Lord Halifax, they announced their intention of building a new European order, but on the whole they created the impression that their chief object was to remove Hitler and his Nazis from the scene and then, so to speak, return to the state of things that existed before the Nazis came into power. But this wouldn't do, and for one excellent reason—namely, that for millions of people all over the world that past—or let us say, the twenty years between the two great wars—simply wasn't good enough. They hadn't liked those years at all, for they had found them undermined by a growing insecurity— both economic and political. They didn't want that world any more. They wanted a changed world. The Nazis were quick to notice this, and put themselves forward, not in their home propaganda, where they were still the fervent nationalists, but in their propaganda abroad, as the revolutionaries who were fighting against the static pluto-democracies—as they called us—in order to change the world. And many people, even though they admired neither the Nazis themselves nor their methods, could not help being influenced by this adroit line of talk. It should have been countered, right from the first, by a declaration that the democracies were even more in favour of a changed world than the Nazis and the Fascists.

I am certain this is true of the British people, it was true of the hundreds and hundreds of serious-minded young soldiers, sailors, airmen, managers and workers, with whom I talked for so many hours, all day and far into the night, during those first months of the war. They regarded the Nazis as I have always regarded them myself—as the greatest obstacle to a new order and a general reform of world conditions. Let's take what is a pretty fair parallel. You have a frontier town that is anxious to clean itself up, to have a decent civic government, to settle its problems of work, wages, housing, health and so on. But in this town a formidable armed gang is operating, and this gang, clearly out for itself, is nevertheless quick to make use of any possible division among the citizens. It tells the rich that it will protect them against the envious poor. It tells the poor that it is working for them against the rich. Now it pretends to be for the employers against the employed, and now for the workers against their masters. And all the time every real move it makes is against all the best common interests of the town and simply in its own

[87]

interest. That is exactly the position of the Nazis in the contemporary world.

And here we may make further use of this parallel. A great deal of anti-democratic capital is now being made out of the fact, which nobody disputes, that totalitarian states organised for war are obviously more efficient—in *wartime*, and please note that—than democratic states are. But what is this supposed to prove? The armed gang in the frontier town will also be more efficient—for their particular purposes, which are blackmail, robbery and murder—than the innocent citizens. But the object of human life is not to make war but to give the fullest possible expression to the human body, mind and soul. If the state is regarded simply as a military engine, then clearly a cast-iron dictatorship is best. But we refuse to regard the state simply as a military engine. It has other and nobler purposes, and for those purposes we believe the democratic system is still the best. Moreover, it can easily be proved that in peacetime these military dictatorships are not efficient at all— that is, they may be manufacturing plenty of guns and airplanes, but the bodily, mental and spiritual health of their citizens is always seen to be declining. Moreover, they *know* they are inefficient on a peace-time basis, and that is one reason why they have always tried to avoid a peace-time basis, have always tried to create an atmosphere in which if war is not actually in being it is at least just round the corner. The reason why the democracies have been so slow and so often out-manoeuvred is the same reason why your decent citizens of a frontier town would appear slow and would at first be often out-manoeuvred by the armed gang. They are trying desperately hard to get on with their ordinary decent lives, and don't want to spend their time swaggering round with pistols in their hands and bumping people off. And our fundamental opposition to the Nazis does not come from the fact that they are Germans who wish to destroy the British Empire, but from the fact that with these gangsters roaring round and holding everybody up, it is simply impossible to get on with a sensible decent civic life at all. Until they are out of the way for good and all, we can make no real progress.

President Roosevelt has done the world a great service by producing, in his Independence Day speech, a list of five freedoms that men must have—freedom from fear and want, freedom of religion, information and expression. And the Nazis represent the denial of all those freedoms. Their own people haven't got them and no people anywhere will have them if the Nazis aren't stopped. That is why it is vitally important that people in the New World should not be lured into believing that this is just another European War. This is a most dangerous belief, which will be encouraged by the Nazi propaganda machine to serve its own ends. This conflict is not just another European War. It is not European. It is not even just another war. Many cynics last September had a good time reminding us that the Great War of 1914-1918 was called the "war to end war"—

"the last war" and so on. And now here was another. But strictly speaking the last war *was* the last war. This conflict, whatever its exact character may be, belongs to quite a different series. It didn't break out because nations quarrelled stupidly about some difference that might have been settled round a conference table. We'd already tried the conference-table method with the Nazis—at Munich—and had seen it brutally and cynically disregarded. No further compromise was possible. These people, the super-armed-gang, were simply determined to go on and on, taking whatever they wanted, and they had to be stopped or life would be no longer worth living. A thousand volumes have not explained clearly yet why the last war broke out. But you could explain this one on a postal card. The issue is plainer than the nose on Hitler's face. And it's no more a European issue than a world outbreak of cholera would be. I can prove that in one sentence. The Nazi organisation is endeavouring to penetrate everywhere on the American continent. Why? For fun? The question answers itself. But though the fundamental issue—which is that the Nazis must be stopped or we simply can't get on with our lives—is plain enough, that isn't to say that all the side issues, all the political and economic and ideological complications, are not elaborate enough, for it is the business of the Nazis to see that they are elaborate, in the hope of confusing opinion everywhere.

Let us uncomplicate it, once and for all. Decent people everywhere—and this includes, I have no doubt, millions of Germans themselves—want to bring order and security, those five freedoms listed by President Roosevelt, into this miserable haunted world, in which man's very inventiveness is being used against his better interests. If we could see those great changes coming, most of us would gladly give our last breath to welcome them. We do not want to live, we do not want our children to live any longer in this vast madhouse. But nothing can be done, not one single great change can be made, no noble world-sweeping reform brought into being, until the menace of these power-crazed Germans is removed and we can set to work in reasonable security. The gang must be broken before the town can be cleaned up. If it is not broken, then we shall go from bad to worse. That is why I believe my own country now arrives at the greatest hour of its destiny. It is now, in the words of a message that recently arrived from a South American state: "the hope of humanity and trustee of the faith of the civilised world."

XIV. This Island Now

July 9, 1940

THERE ARE two corrections I want to make to current Nazi propaganda. First, air raids. There has been a great deal of German raiding lately, but the results, so far from being effective, either as regards military objectives or civilian morale, have been so negligible that the general opinion here has been that these raids can only have been feelers, attempts to discover where the best defences are located. This may be a compliment to the German Air Force that it doesn't deserve, and possibly, by assuming that these are "feelers" rather than serious big raids, we may be under-estimating our really formidable defences; but we are so anxious not to be complacent that we are ready to assume that so far the Nazis are not really trying. We find it impossible to believe that this tip-and-run raiding, with bombs by the score falling into the sea or on waste ground or failing to explode, can really be Goering in action.

Speaking of Goering, I had a note this morning from a librarian, who tells me that yesterday a woman came into her library and took out Singer's book called *Goering, Germany's Most Dangerous Man,* and said that she'd take it out "just for a bit of fun." You can call that an example of our British complacency, if you like; but, out of a very good knowledge of our character, I would call it a good example of that curious element, half humorous and half defiant, which is completely unknown to the earnest, anxious, worried German type of mind, an element that the Nazis don't understand and that—in the long run—will beat them.

Notice, too, the behaviour of that farmer's wife who was told that a Nazi parachutist was landing on her farm. Actually he was a Nazi airman whose machine had just been destroyed. She marched out to him—though he was a fellow over six feet tall—and told him to put up his hands, then made him give her his revolver. She then marched him into her yard, where a few moments later soldiers on motorcycles arrived and claimed their prisoner. Now of course we know that a real parachutist would behave differently from an airman who had just baled out, but the point of the story is not the behaviour of the Nazi but the behaviour of the farmer's wife.

Here again, I discover this element that the Nazis can't take into proper account because they simply don't understand it. We can't tell, of course, what part it would play in an attempted invasion, but my own feeling is that it would play a very great part indeed, that it's already playing a great part, because the reply of the British people to this gigantic bogey-bogey propaganda of the Nazi screaming machine is not to wonder and mutter in corners but to raise their voices in defiance and dare them to do their damnedest. A week or two ago, there were half a million local defence volunteers, now there are over a million. That's the spirit I mean.

People are very funny about the soldiers, because on this island we're not used to seeing a lot of troops about, with the result that now people solemnly tell you that in *their* particular district, which they obviously feel has been singled out for special attention, there are astonishing numbers of troops. What they don't realise, of course, is that the same can be said of every other district, because for the very first time in its whole history this island is now garrisoned by a large army, which is being added to now at the rate of seven thousand recruits a day. This army at the moment stands on the defensive, waiting for Hitler to fulfil all his threats, but if Hitler should decide to leave us alone, that does not mean that these gigantic military preparations are, so to speak, left up in the air, for the spirit of this army is fundamentally *offensive*, not merely *defensive*. This island is not only a garrison now but it might also be called the camp of a vast crusade, the last and greatest of the crusades, to redeem from the infidel the holy sepulchre of man's free spirit. There is now a fantastic mingling of the fighting men of numerous nations. There are, first, the men from our Dominions —husky sun-tanned Canadians, Australians, New Zealanders—and other tough fighting men from the ends of the earth. Then there are the foreign legions of defiant free men—there are French soldiers, airmen, sailors, there are Poles, there are Czechs, Dutch, Norwegians. Isn't there something grand and heartening about all this? To know that this small island, now bristling with defiance, is the rallying point of all the fighting forces of freedom everywhere, to know that we're living in the vast camp of this last and noblest crusade, to know that here men can still laugh at the vain antics of that crazy tyrant. I haven't been proud of my country for years, as anybody who knows my books will readily agree. But—by thunder!—I am now, and though I'm no hero—in fact at this late day I'd put myself well down among the cowards—I wouldn't be anywhere else for a fortune.

My second correction concerns food. There is to be further rationing. I am glad of it, and have been saying in private this last week or two that there ought, as a matter of public policy, to be more rationing. The point is, that as a people we are not—and never have been—very wise about food, and we share this weakness with the whole Anglo-Saxon race. We have two faults. These two faults are that we are both too wasteful and too conservative. I have always thought that in both Britain and America we have suffered, as cooks, simply because there has always been far too much easy good raw material about. We have never learned—and I take this to be the basis of the art of cookery—to make the very most of what we have. For example, I'm extremely fond of soups, and when I dine in a restaurant where I know the soups are good, I always order a soup. But the average English cook or housewife simply won't trouble to make good soup, and I'm hoping that now she'll have to try, and that perhaps after this war I may find myself in a much better world but thoroughly "in the soup." People here won't experiment with dishes, not so much, I think, because the women are lazy as that their menfolk, not being much interested in food, wouldn't like experiment. And they're all wrong, because gastronomic experiment, even if it lands you with frogs and snails and queer fungi, is as valuable as it is exciting. Again, the English—especially the working folk—have a passion for snacks, in which bread and butter and cups of tea play a great part. And if the new rationing is going to cut down this habit, which in my opinion is a bad habit, then so much the better. My own feeling for some time—and I'm a man with a hearty appetite—has been that the authorities should have interfered much more with the customary modes of feeding here, not only for the sake of cutting down shipping space, but also because smaller rations of such things as tea and all the sweet and starchy stuff would lead to a definite improvement in our way of living. Actually, compared with the last war, this one doesn't know what shortage means, and at this moment I'd say that the average consumption of most necessary food-stuffs here is far far greater than it has been in most European countries at any time during the last fifty years.

The other day, dining with some friends, I met a cultivated German-Jewish woman, who at the mere suggestion that there was any real food rationing here simply roared with laughter, and said we hadn't the least idea what rationing meant. And I must say that I have never at any time been proud of our Anglo-Saxon wastefulness and stupid conservatism in this matter of food, and if the war, by compelling us to take an intelligent interest in the kitchen, turns us into a nation of decent cooks it will have achieved something.

What a day that would be! No more Nazis, and good soups and salads and properly cooked vegetables on every British table—oh happy day!

XV. Comic Fairy Tales from Berlin

July 11, 1940

I HAVE DISCUSSED Nazi propaganda in its wider, more sinister and more successful aspects, showing how the Nazis go from country to country encouraging opposition in each country to any party that is hostile to them, pretending to be friends of the rich in one place and friends of the poor in another, changing their colour whenever it should be necessary, and above all encouraging everywhere those men whom they recognise to be of the same psychological type as themselves, men who will do anything for power. In this kind of propaganda, which has been always backed by plenty of hard cash, the Nazis have been very successful. But when we come to a more topical and intimate type of propaganda, we notice at once that they are far less successful, almost dead failures. And for a very good reason. The Nazis at home are by this time used to dealing with an exceptionally credulous and foolish public, who almost ask to be taken away from reality—and whether they ask for it or not *are* taken away from reality and told ridiculous fairy tales. We shouldn't be surprised that the German people are now like that, for the whole aim of Nazi education, if it can fairly be called education, is to abolish the least glimmer of any critical intelligence, and the doubters and scoffers, who refuse to be hoodwinked, have either been sent into exile, taken to concentration camps or bullied into silence. The rest of their public simply asks to be taken in, to be doped with lies and nonsense, to live in a mental Cloud Cuckoodom.

Having this silly and easy public to handle at home, the Nazi propagandists who deal with topical and more intimate stuff are simply too careless and slapdash in their propaganda of this sort for abroad. With the not unpleasant result that some of the best laughs we get come from the labours of these solemn idiots. For example, this week they have been telling the world about what is happening in London. Nothing could be more fantastic than their accounts of this London that they've invented.

In this London of theirs, for instance, we're told that "people are providing themselves with private machine-gun nests." I'd like to see the face of an officer of our Royal Ordnance Corps if a private citizen came to him and asked for armaments for a private machine-gun nest. But that is only the beginning. They can do much better than that. "There are," they tell us, "riots in London every night, and it is getting impossible to live in town." Where these nightly riots are, who joins in them, we aren't told, but I am out nearly every night, and return home at all hours, and I've yet to see anything that looked remotely like a riot. Perhaps their spies listen-in to conversations they don't understand, and hearing one theatrical manager telling another that

[99]

his new musical show is a riot they jump to the conclusion that the populace must be rioting.

Then the world has just been told by these Nazi experts that "the slightest criticism in England is punished by deportation." All I can say to that is that if the slightest criticism is so severely punished, then some of us, who indulge in criticism that is far from being slight, must have been shot long since and simply don't know it. It is announced also that "A number of persons have been sentenced to five years' imprisonment for tuning in to German stations." That's an interesting example of the Nazi mentality. Now, in Germany—and not only in Germany but in all those unhappy territories under Nazi rule, in Norway, the Low Countries, in two-thirds of France—listening to foreign broadcasts is punished by severe penalties, imprisonment and even worse. Everybody knows that. If the English Government behaved in the same monstrous fashion, the Nazis ought to be the last people in the world to blame them. They would be only doing now what the Nazis have been doing for a long time. But actually, of course, everybody in this country is perfectly free to listen to any broadcasting station he chooses, and nobody has ever been even locked up for five minutes—never mind five years' imprisonment—for listening to German broadcasts. We think that listening to German propaganda carries its own punishment with it—that of being treated as if you were a credulous child by some dreary traitor, who's compelled to advertise his treachery to the very people he's ratted on.

But the Nazis can do better even than these thumping lies. Here's a beauty: "All British newspapers are to be abolished, and an official gazette to be published." There again, you have the same trick, to pretend that what has happened already in Germany is now happening in Britain. For though there are a number of newspapers published in Germany, for all practical purposes they are merely variations of an official gazette, there being no freedom of the press. No British newspapers are being abolished. Even the communist paper, the *Daily Worker*, which curses nearly everything the Government ever does, still comes out and may be bought in the streets.

And now we come to one that has at least a suggestion of the truth about it. "The whole British nation," it begins, "has taken to drink." Well, there's something in that, but we'd taken to drink, of some sort or other, long before the Nazis were heard of, and will, I'm convinced, still be saying "Cheerio" to each other and taking our liquor when the Nazis are nothing but an evil memory. Then after announcing that we've all taken to drink, they go on to say "Never were there seen so many drunken people in London as now." Here this propagandist in Berlin has the advantage of me, for I just happen to live here and move about all hours of day and night, and just happen not to see all these drunks. You have to get as far away as Berlin to see this orgy going on in London every night. Just living here, right on the spot, I can only say that I never saw *less* drunkenness. But I'll promise this propagandist this much, that sooner or later there *will* come a night when it will seem as if all London's drunk, not with liquor but with happiness. But neither this fellow nor his Nazi employers will be in a position then to comment upon this night, because it will be celebrating their total and final disappearance from the world.

And now here is, I think, my favourite: "The fear of German planes is terrific. One of the best proofs of this is that the Jews are having their hair dyed and their noses straightened."

It's a shame to spoil that exquisite invention even by commenting on it. Let's just leave it, and imagine that Oxford Street and Regent Street and Piccadilly and Bond Street and the Strand are now filled with shops in which Jews are having their hair dyed and their noses straightened. The whole West End is crowded with people who have bright golden hair and very straight noses. The rest of us, not being busy with hair-dying and nose-straightening, have nothing else to do but to suffer from this terrific fear of German planes. You can't hear yourself speak in the streets for the chattering of teeth and the knocking of knees. Everybody is so terrified in London that you see the people every night crowding into restaurants and eating and drinking and laughing and dancing, pushing their way into theatres and film shows, hiding themselves in ice-skating and roller-skating rinks, at whist drives or greyhound racing, listening to music or watching the ballet, and at the week-end going to tennis courts and golf links. I tell you, the panic is awful. At least, that's how it looks from Berlin.

Here in London it isn't quite so obvious. I was talking this afternoon to a young American journalist, who had only landed here, paying us his first visit, a week or two ago. *He* told me, though of course he couldn't possibly know as much about it as these people in Berlin, that he'd been staggered by the cheerful calm of the folk here, which seemed almost restful after the huge headlines and the excitement about the war in New York. In fact he paid us a lot of nice compliments, which I'd better not repeat, for we're generally supposed to be a conceited lot, for ever pleased with ourselves, but not given to displaying our bouquets in public.

Now for the supreme effort of this week's Nazi propaganda, which is this: "Panic in Britain is so great that millions are leaving the country." For sheer impudence, this has never been beaten so far in the war. Consider the statement that millions—*millions*—are leaving this country. Where are they going to, these millions? And how are they going, these millions? Taking a very modest estimate of "millions," let us say there are two million people involved. Now there are only two ways of leaving this country, either by passenger plane or by ship. It would take at least 40,000 passenger planes to remove two million persons, far far more big passenger planes than exist in the whole world. It would take a thousand first-class large liners to remove these same people by sea, far far more first-class large liners than exist in the whole world. Then these millions cannot have left this island either by air or by sea, and they certainly haven't been walking away from it, so how have they gone? This statement that millions are leaving this country is no more false than the one that precedes it, that panic here is so great.

There are no millions leaving, there is no panic. It is all wretched drivel, so obviously silly that the only persons who would ever waste their time putting such stuff on the air are persons who have come to the conclusion that all other people will believe any rubbish. This comes of handling a home public that has long since said goodbye to criticism and to free speech. It is the natural result of taking as their bible *Mein Kampf*, which boldly states that human beings are so silly that you have only to keep on repeating huge lies to have them believed.

And now, having had enough comic fairy tales, let us take a brief look at London as it really is, after ten months of war. To my mind, it is a far less depressing city than it was during the first months of the war, when I found the complete black-out and the sudden switch-over to wartime conditions rather melancholy. In those days, you were always missing your friends, wondering what had become of them. Now you are always discovering them again, and celebrating the meeting with a modest little party. I don't know what restaurants in general are like, these nights, but I know that my own favourite—the Ivy—where I entertained some friends last night, is usually pretty full. The moving-picture theatres are doing fairly good business. The ordinary theatres have slumped, many of the leading players being on tour, and many of us naturally shrink from putting on new plays at this time. Then all the nations of Europe are gathering here. Thus, my wife, who is a good linguist and so is often called upon to help with billeting, was busy the other day with the wives of Polish officers, and today was equally busy billeting women and little babies from Malta. And everybody is busy producing unwanted household stores of aluminium—Americans call it "al*um*inum"—pots and pans and lemon squeezers and other utensils, because there is a temporary shortage of this metal for aircraft construction.

I don't know what the total result of this collection will be, but it looks like being very useful. I know our hall this afternoon seemed to be bristling with piles of white metal pots and pans. Somebody has found a good slogan: "Your pan will help to cook Hitler's goose," and on that cheerful mixed note, which combines the homely domestic with the whole world problem, and does not, I trust, suggest panic or millions leaving the country in fleets of invisible planes and ships, I will conclude.

XVI. British Children—
the Problem of Evacuation

July 14, 1940

AN HOUR or two ago, a boy delivered a cable to us, and it was from our friends, the Roark Bradfords, in New Orleans, asking us to send two of our children to them. Similar cables have been arriving at our house every other day or so, for weeks. We used to stay on Jack Burden's ranch at Wickenburg, Arizona, and the other day we had a cable from him telling us to send the whole family and he'd look after them on the ranch. For all these offers—and I know how many English families have received them lately—we're all more than grateful, we're deeply moved. Whatever happens, if not another child can be evacuated, our hearts will be stirred and warmed for years by the thought of how magnificently the people overseas responded to this suggestion of evacuating our children. There is in the New World a tradition of instant, warm-hearted hospitality, but surely that tradition has never shone more brightly than it has done in these dark days. This is a time when generosity and pity and firm friendship rise gloriously above the mass of fear and hate and corruption like great blossoming trees above a dark swamp.

And now let us consider this problem of evacuating our children. For me it's anything but an abstract problem, for in my own family there are six children, and four of them are within the suggested age limits of evacuation. Our Prime Minister, when he told the House of Commons, the other day, what had happened to the French Fleet, said that when the question came up about attacking the French Fleet if it refused to surrender or go to a neutral port, the Cabinet had the hardest decision to make that any British Cabinet has ever had to make. But for the last weeks—and in some instances, my own for one, for the past ten months—fathers and mothers of children here have been faced with the task of making an even more difficult decision, a terrible and heart-rending task. They have had to decide whether to keep their children here, where the blitzkrieg might decend upon them at any moment, or break up the family and let them sail the dangerous seas to the other side of the world, where they might have to remain perhaps for years. If you kept them here, and all hell broke loose, then you would never stop blaming yourself for not having got them away. On the other hand, if you sent them away and their ship was torpedoed, you would curse the hour you let them go. And even if they crossed the seas safely, and you knew, as we all do know, what generosity and affection would reach them in their new life, you would feel that half your heart and mind were at the other side of the world, that your family had been broken up for good and all, that your children might grow up to be strangers to you.

I tell you, there never was a more diabolically diffi-

cult problem for parents to solve. We've had months
and months of argument about it, with all our friends
who have children. When it was first announced that
the Government might take steps to evacuate young children overseas, my wife was still living in our house in
the country, and the simple women from the village and
the farms around came to her to ask her advice as to
what they should do, and she told me soon afterwards
how heart-breaking it was to witness their pitiful bewilderment and their anxiety to do what was best for
their children. Nothing, she said, had ever moved her
so much as these simple decent mothers, their eyes
heavy with tears, asking her to tell them what to do.
Good God!—when we think of the misery brought to
such decent simple folk all over Europe, perhaps soon
all over the world, by these power-crazed Nazis and
their hordes of screaming demented lads, it makes us
wonder why the whole world doesn't rise up in its
wrath and put an end to these lunatics once and for all.
All this patter about neutrality and non-belligerency is
like sitting down and doing crossword puzzles in front
of a pack of ravening wolves. But there was our terrible
problem—the children.

If we had wanted to get our own children away to
America, my wife and I were in a fortunate position, for
our children had already been twice for long visits to
America, we had many good friends there who were
ready to look after them, and because of American
royalties on my books and plays, the financial question

was easier for us. But until there was a general scheme for evacuating children overseas, I felt I couldn't take advantage of my fortunate position, because I felt that I couldn't spend my time, as I do, both on the air and in the press, asking ordinary folk to be of good heart and to fight the Nazis to the end, if my children had been sent away to safety and theirs hadn't. Clearly that wasn't good enough. You may say that the same criticism can be applied to many of the parents, some of them holding high government offices, whose children have recently arrived in New York. But this is not so, because those children were sent after it was commonly understood that everybody who applied would have a chance to get their children away, when it could no longer be considered a class issue. It must be clearly understood too, that there is a difference, from the official point of view, between the government scheme of evacuation and the private dispatch of children by their parents as ordinary passengers to America. The difference is that, with the government scheme of evacuation, the Government would have to take full responsibility for the safety of the children while at sea, whereas if children go in the ordinary way, as private passengers, they do so purely at their parents' own risk. Now, as you all know, the scheme has been held up because the Government feels that the necessary measures to ensure the safe passage of these most precious cargoes would make too many and great demands at this time on our naval resources. You may be sure that this decision was not lightly arrived at. The disappointment so many Americans are feeling is shared by thousands here. But we must face the grim realities of the situation. There is nothing in the Nazis' record so far to suggest that they would allow ships crowded with children to pass in safety. These are the people who have never hesitated to threaten their own fellow-countrymen by using their families as hostages. These are the people who have torpedoed innocent passenger ships without warning, time after time. These are the people who in Belgium and northern France deliberately drove millions of old persons, women and children down the roads, bombing and machine-gunning them as they went, merely in order to confuse and impede the opposing armies. These are the people who carefully waited until all defences had been withdrawn from the Channel Isles, and then—brave fellows!—ruthlessly bombed the defenceless civilians who remained. No scruples of mercy and decency have ever restrained them yet, and to imagine that they will now, when their screams of fury at Britain, their last and greatest and most indomitable enemy, are rising higher and higher, is dangerous wishful thinking.

Let us face the fact, which ought to be obvious enough by now, that it is not flags and idle talk of neutrality, it is not mercy, chivalry, kindness, decency, that will ever stop the Nazis from releasing a bomb or a torpedo, it is only the fierce onslaught of our terrible fighting planes, the warning bark of anti-aircraft guns, the grim menace of the long grey ships of the Navy, the challenge of stout-hearted fighting men, that will put a stop to their cruel antics. It was a noble thought— and we honour all those who support it—to send ships over for the children, but what we want more than those ships are machines and devices of war. Then though the evil Swastika flies from North Cape to Finisterre, we'll go on and on until in the end we break their damned hearts. Yes, even if it means keeping the children. We don't want our children mixed up in a blitzkrieg, although certain facts coming to light now do suggest that the situation is not as bad as it first appeared, for we have a good deal of evidence, which has careful medical authority behind it, that children as a whole stand the strain of continued bombing raids better than adults do, their natures being more resilient and better able to repair any serious loss of sleep. The younger ones are quickly adaptive, and the older ones, who know what is happening, do not for the most part —I can speak for my own and my friends' children— show any urgent desire to find safety out of the country. It is only when adults show obvious traces of panic that children begin to suffer, and the British people do not propose to show any traces of panic or to feel panic-stricken.

I repeat, we don't want our children to endure a blitzkrieg, but still less—and here I'm sure I speak for all British parents—do we want them to live, whether here or overseas makes no difference, in a world dominated by the Nazis, in a world sold into slavery by these latter-day Mongols and Huns. They were brought up to be free and laughter-loving and civilised, and sooner than see them enslaved, miserable, and serving such evil barbaric masters, we'd rather have them die with us.

XVII. A Glimpse into
Broadcasting House

July 16, 1940

L ET ME take you into Broadcasting House, from which
I regularly speak. Such a glimpse should be regarded as a friendly privilege since the place is very
securely guarded these days, and to enter it it is necessary
to carry various passes and permits.

Floor after floor is crowded with broadcasting studios
and offices, many of which are busy day and night. Often
as I pass down a corridor, I see through the little round
windows let into the door of each studio one foreign
face after another leaning towards the microphone; and
in the elevators, along the landings or in the restaurant,
I hear the speech of all nations, and see uniforms and
medal ribbons that are as strange to me as those of
Ruritania. Very often I feel as if I were travelling,
perhaps out into space, towards some happier planet, in
a vast ship of all the nations, in some modern Ark. And
really that's not so fanciful either, because this Broadcasting House is now the last home of free speech in
Western Europe. I don't mean we haven't a censor-
ship, of course we have; you're bound to have one in
a war, if only to avoid giving the intelligence departments of the enemy a lot of valuable information. But
compared with what they have in the rest of Western

[113]

Europe, with the Gestapo looking over their shoulders, you can say we have positively wild free speech here. And we provide for many of the conquered peoples their last link with the outside world.

Day and night, news bulletins and talks go out from this building to those people in their own languages. Altogether more than twenty languages are used for news bulletins and talks. This is not only the modern Ark but also another Tower of Babel. One of the most elaborate services is to the Germans themselves. There is a special early-morning broadcast chiefly intended for German workers. There is a mid-day bulletin, mainly addressed to the professional classes. Another at two-thirty for German women. Then later at night special talks and news services in German. Included among these are selections from actual recordings of Hitler's speeches. You may be surprised that we broadcast Hitler's speeches to the Germans, but we do this to show how he has constantly contradicted himself and broken his promises. If we merely *said* he had, German listeners might not believe us, but we give them these actual recordings of his speeches, made at the time he spoke, and so convict him of prolonged deceit out of his own mouth. (You can understand why the Nazis threaten anybody who listens to our broadcasts with terrible penalties.) Then the Czech programmes have been very successful. I met a Czech general here, the other night, who had just been talking to his own folk over the air. These programmes are also used to enable men in the various Allied forces here to announce to their families far away that they are alive and well. One of the most successful used to be called the "Polish Agony Column," which did very valuable service—it only stopped about a week ago—establishing the whereabouts of thousands of Polish soldiers, sailors, airmen, and passing on this urgent information. We are now doing this for the French soldiers and sailors, and only last night I heard a most moving thing.

What happens is this. The B.B.C. sends round a recording van to the hospitals where these wounded Frenchmen are being cared for, and the men then make a record, reciting in turn their names and rank, where they live when at home, and then sending a brief message to their families. These records are included in the French programme from Broadcasting House, and you can hear these men sending their little messages home —some eager and happy, others shy and diffident, others again mournful, remembering all that has happened to their beloved France. To me this mere recital of their names and their brief greetings, by these simple men in their own gruff voices, was infinitely more moving than the most eloquent talks about the fall of France. They followed it last night by that monotonous popular French music which you might hear in any little cabaret or even bistro in Montmartre, and that touch of nostalgic gaiety just about completed the heartbreak of the whole thing.

Well, that's what is happening in Broadcasting

House. I pop in at nearly all times, and often have to stay until nearly all times, and it always seems to be going in pretty full swing—with the little red lights in the studios winking and then burning steadily, with typewriters hammering away at scripts in the rows and rows of offices, loud speakers booming away in corners, young men with untidy hair and pipes in their mouths bursting in and out of conferences, neat waitresses in black-and-white uniforms from the restaurant carrying trays, charming girl secretaries arriving all spick-and-span or departing looking rather wilted, the fellows up in the news room, most of them former newspaper-men, sitting in shirtsleeves and wearing eyeshades as if this were really a Hollywood newspaper film, important personages in every kind of uniform making for the director general's room, and late at night the B.B.C.'s own local defence volunteers making the rounds with their guns. And somewhere behind all this, taking this vast stream of talk and information in twenty different languages and spraying it round the world, is a vast and mightily efficient engineering staff, but who they are, how and where they do it, I haven't the foggiest notion, for I never remember setting eyes on one of them. But the final impression is not that of an enormous and super-efficient organisation, a marvellous machine of communication, though it is all that, but of a large group of men and women who belong to many different nations and may have come from the ends of the earth to work within these high white walls, but who are all united by a sense of common purpose, and by a stout defiance of all tyranny and by a deep pity for all those who are suffering because they have now lost their ancient liberties.

XVIII. Two Moot Points: The Burma Road and the British Blockade

July 21, 1940

DURING the last few days, America has been having a very good share of the front pages of newspapers here. First, there was the Democratic Convention and the nomination of Mr. Roosevelt for a third term. Then there were the American reactions to Hitler's speech, which, as usual, were very prominently displayed. Indeed, anybody who judged from our newspapers would very much over-estimate the general public interest here in American opinion.

I don't mean for a moment to suggest that people here are indifferent to American opinion; they aren't; they are nearly always interested to learn what America is thinking. But they're not so excited about it as the newspapers might lead an outsider to think. They're not all panting to know what America thinks of Hitler's speech, and I don't think I've heard the American reaction more than casually mentioned in talk. As far as the other topic, the Presidential election, is concerned, the trouble here is that the mass of the people don't understand American politics—in spite of Mr. Raymond Gram Swing's excellent radio talks—and also they don't know the various political personalities that are emerging in this campaign. They know and very much like Mr. Roosevelt, for of course they have seen and heard him many many times on the news reels here, as well as hearing his voice on the air, and he has the kind of personality that can put itself over even in such brief glimpses of it. But the others, including Mr. Willkie, they know little or nothing about. Then again, it's very hard for anybody living outside the United States to understand American politics, if only because the two great American political parties don't seem to express permanent and universal attitudes of mind, such as reactionary, on the one side, and radical and progressive, on the other. In most countries, you have a pretty good idea what the Right, the Centre and the Left parties will stand for. But the American division into Republicans and Democrats is either too simple or too complicated for outsiders to understand; and although I know American life and American history, I must confess that I'm frequently bewildered. So you can imagine that most of our folk here just give it up.

The attitude here towards America is extremely interesting. You would imagine sometimes from the attention our press pays to American opinion that the people here were just waiting for America to join us in this war and could hardly think about anything else. But actually it is hardly ever mentioned. I can't say anything about our politicians, but I do know that the British people aren't waiting for anybody to rescue them, but for the time being are just doggedly going about their preparations to meet any attempt at inva-

sion, feeling—at this moment, anyhow—self-contained
and rather self-content. We're so used, as a people, to
sending out expeditionary forces all over the world,
that it's a new sensation for us to wait on our island to
see what the Nazis think they can do. "All right then,
come on and do it," the people are saying, and they're
not much concerned about American opinion. Later, of
course, that may change. But on the other hand, I hear
none of those sneers and jeers at America that I remember in 1916. The isolationists aren't particularly
admired, but the people here who are interested realise
that it takes time for people to lose old habits of
thought. Two years ago, we'd plenty of isolationists
here—all the newspapers formerly controlled by Lord
Beaverbrook, for example, were strongly isolationist,
and took the line that Britain is not an European power,
should not concern itself with European affairs, but
should look to the Empire. This is, of course, the
ostrich sticking its head in the sand, but then so is all
isolationism. It's foolish because it denies the most obvious fact about the modern world, and that is the complete interdependence of all its parts. Isolationism is
really taking a mental rocket to the moon. It just won't
work, as our isolationists here soon found out. And the
most fatal thing to do with this present conflict is to
try and give it boundaries. *It is a world conflict.* And
it came into existence not because of a few events in
Central Europe, but because the world has recently
seen the end of one system, which lasted for about a

hundred and fifty years, and is now trying to decide which system will succeed it.

To imagine that the United States has no direct interest in this world upheaval is like pretending in an earthquake that you may only be feeling a trifle giddy. But I don't find any *impatience* here about America. It's only now and again when the journalists and commentators start *lecturing* us from a high moral standpoint that we're apt to become rather impatient. For example, about this closing of the Burma Road. Now for my part, speaking entirely as a private citizen, I don't like this temporary agreement with Japan about the Burma Road. It's another little dose of that useless medicine—appeasement. Like all liberals here, I reserve all my sympathies for China, and indeed I have a really profound admiration for these modern Chinese, with their indomitable guerilla armies, their new co-operative industries, their refusal to allow any side of their corporate life to be destroyed by the Japanese in-vaders. I know something about the Chinese struggle, and also about the sympathy with it here, because last summer I edited a large pamphlet, made up to look like an illustrated magazine, called *China News*. I could quote attacks upon the Burma Road agreement that have been published in the press this week-end. But, to be quite candid, I do feel that criticism of this move comes better from us here than from American com-mentators, who never succeeded in stopping the sale of American munitions to Japan, and seem to have made up their minds that it is just as wrong for Britain to refuse to fight all the aggressive powers on earth as it is wrong for the United States to fight aggression at all.

One of our most conservative papers is the *Sunday Observer*, which has often rebuked us liberals and radicals for our wild words. But even the *Sunday Observer* says today of the Burma Road agreement: "A final just settlement in the Far East is impossible except jointly by the five powers, Japan, China, Britain, the United States, and Russia. Japan presents a menace to China, and thereby also to Britain, the United States and Russia. Britain is engaged in a life and death struggle in the West. She fights alone, though she fights the battle of all free peoples. The issue in the Far East is postponed only. In its turn it will be settled." That is worth pondering on, though, I repeat, it does not entirely represent my own point of view.

A week or two ago, I suggested that very soon Nazi propaganda would be making great use of the "poor starving Europe" theme. And now this is happening already. Let's see what the game is. The Nazi propaganda line is this. Germany has just enough food for herself, and so can defy the British blockade, but all these poor countries under her control are already suffering—and soon will suffer much worse—all because of the wicked British. Now let's look at the facts. All these countries—Norway, Denmark, Holland, Belgium, France—were exceptionally well provided with food-stuffs before Germany broke in and robbed their larders. Of all the countries in Europe, these happen to be the ones that were well provided for, some of them, like Denmark and Holland, being exporters of dairy produce and the like. But now, it seems, after a month or two of German occupation, these same countries are rapidly drawing near to destitution. Why? The answer is obvious. Because Germany, without the least thought for the immediate future of these unhappy peoples, proceeded at once to loot everything edible, slaughtered cattle and pigs by the hundred thousand, and swept the cupboard bare. It's just good old looting on a vast scale. The grey-coated hordes have descended upon Western Europe like a gigantic plague of locusts. Now, having grabbed everything they could lay their hands on, they are pretending to feel sorry for their wretched victims, and are whining about our blockade.

Now a word about our blockade, the object of which isn't always understood. The object of a blockade is not, as some people seem to imagine, the reduction of an enemy by starving his women and children. What a blockade does is to give the enemy a choice between reducing his military effort, that is, taking people away from the army and making munitions and airplanes and putting them to the task of producing more food, or alternatively of keeping up the maximum military effort by putting everybody on very short rations. In the last war, the Germans went short of food simply because their commanders always gambled throughout the war on a military victory and therefore put the needs of the army before those of the civilian population. They said, in effect, "Guns before butter." Four years ago, when there was no British blockade and Germany could acquire all the food she wanted, the Nazis publicly announced that their policy was "Guns before butter." It was their own policy, and had nothing to do with any British blockade. But of course what they had in their mind was this, that once they had the guns, they'd soon find some butter, and now they have found some, but they want some more, not for themselves, of course, but for the poor Norwegians, Danes, Dutch, Belgians, French, who seem to be mysteriously short of all the good things they had a few weeks ago. Meanwhile, the Nazi policy is, of course, more and more guns, to bully everybody with, to go racketeering with, to assist what is now their national industry— robbery under arms. And our blockade is still, at this very moment, the best weapon the world possesses with which to resist this vast threatening tyranny. Remove that line of grey weatherbeaten ships, and the lifeline of human liberty has gone.

XIX. Wartime London, in Sharply Contrasted Phases

July 25, 1940

AFTER suffering a cold for several days I went out this afternoon to keep two engagements, which are interesting because they offer two sharply contrasted pictures of this wartime life of ours in London.

The first engagement was to speak at a very big garden fête that was being held in a London suburb in aid of funds for the blind. Following a suggestion I had made some weeks ago on the air about the need for more bands and flags and high jinks generally, the promoters of this fête had arranged for a big community singing accompanied by a good band. So my job was to give this a start, not—thank goodness—by singing, but by telling the crowd, which was very large and enthusiastic, that it would do us all good to sing. I told them that this was either a people's war or it was nothing, and that the people wanted to set about it in their own fashion, ready to fight and work like blazes and never to give in, but at the same time trying to make the best of life as they went along, enjoying every bit of colour, fun, beauty, that comes their way. I said that if we were compelled to make our own minds as dreary, gloomy and fanatical as Hitler's, then we'd given him the victory. But that if on top of that dogged

resolution which has always been a notable character-
istic of the British, we build high shining towers of
humour and music and cheerful comradeship, then we
completely defy him and his ant-like hordes and at the
same time enjoy our own way of life. I said, "Let the
people sing." And they did, rolling their choruses above
the band, singing

> "Bring me my bow of burning gold,
> Bring me my arrows of desire,
> Bring me my spear: O clouds unfold,
> Bring me my chariot of fire. . . ."

What a picture it was—the crowd round the little
amphitheatre above the rosebushes, the lawns stretch-
ing away, the soft foliage beyond, and above, the
silvery barrage balloons against the sky. It was real
community singing and it gave me a proper sense of
community. This sense of community is beginning to
be very deeply felt here, and I believe that it can be
used not merely to preserve the liberties of our people
and to destroy the Nazis but also to build up a far
nobler Britain than the world has yet seen.

My second engagement took me to a group of men,
all of intellectual distinction, who are already planning
the new post-war world, working out all the complicated problems of the distribution of raw materials, industrial methods, nutrition, housing, and education.
There couldn't have been a sharper contrast to the great
crowd roaring out their choruses with the brass band in
the garden than this quiet group of intellectuals sitting

round a table, pooling their ideas and their research. Each has some important job to do for most of the day and sometimes half the night, but in their spare time they work away at these problems, meet regularly round this table to shape and polish their conclusions, and every now and then produce an important memorandum. There are probably a dozen such groups in this city—though not all as distinguished as this particular group—quietly meeting to try and see ahead, to sort out the complicated facts, to free their minds from prejudice, to work out new techniques, to plan the cities and towns and villages and workshops of the future Britain.

So there you have two sharply contrasted phases of this wartime London that the Nazis tell us is in a state of panic. Aren't these people of London taking the war in the right spirit? Not just enduring all the restrictions and the rationing and the barrage of threats by the Nazis, but all in their several different ways making the most of the moment, not living, as one might imagine, only about half the life they led a year ago, but really living a much fuller and richer life. There is a grand neighbourliness about these folk now. The divisions between classes—always England's weakness—are being rapidly rubbed out. People of all kinds are ready to help. It's that sense of community again, and if we can't make something grand out of it, Hitler or no Hitler, then we deserve all we shall get. But I hope, I believe, we shall.

XX. "Less Bread and More Taxes"

July 28, 1940

THE REACTION to the new budget here has been very significant. Here is a budget that raises the income tax to eight-and-sixpence in the pound—that is, to forty-two-point-five per cent. It lowers the scale at which surtax begins, increases the rate of that tax very sharply, so that even a moderately rich man—not a very rich man—will soon find himself paying ninety per cent of his income in taxes. Then it raises the duties on things like tobacco, beer, wines. Britain is very hard on her smokers, who always seem to me to pay more than their share of taxes. Why, tobacco is now four times the price it was when I first started smoking. And the duty on whisky is now so high that a friend of mine, who is very fond of his glass of Scotch, has publicly announced that buying a bottle of whisky is almost like buying a government savings bond, so much of the price goes back to the national exchequer. Then in addition to these various increases, the new budget proposes—very unwisely, most of us think—to clap a tax of twenty-four per cent on a great many semi-luxury articles, and half that tax, twelve per cent, on many other articles, including books, periodicals, newspapers.

I find it hard to believe, myself, that this tax on information, knowledge, ideas, culture, will ever be allowed to come into operation. And for that reason it clashes badly with the avowed object of this purchase tax, which exists not so much to raise revenue as to check expenditure on what are regarded as unnecessary articles. But I can hardly believe that the Chancellor of the Exchequer wishes to cut down the sales of books, periodicals, newspapers, that he thinks there should be less information, less knowledge, fewer ideas, less culture.

Here then is this interim budget—"interim" because it has been brought out between the regular budgets and so may be regarded as temporary and supplementary—which imposes the most gigantic financial burden known to this or any other free people. By comparison with anything known before, it is staggering. If Victorian statesmen like Gladstone could be brought back to learn what taxes are now being successfully imposed on the British people, they would never believe their ears. Yet—and this is the significant thing—this budget has been unfavourably received everywhere, not because it asks too much—*but because it doesn't ask enough*. In one of Lewis Carroll's fantastic tales—I think it is *Sylvie and Bruno*—he makes a crowd get together and shout "Less bread and more taxes." But now, in this new wonderland of the 1940's, that is more or less what *is* being shouted here: "Less bread and more taxes." Newspapers at each end of the political scale, from the Tories to the Socialists, declare emphatically that this budget doesn't go far enough. The

Chancellor should demand much more. The Government, which *starts* its direct taxation at nearly half of what we earn and has piled on indirect taxation, is accused of timidity. "Come on," people cry, "you can do better than that." There is a very vivid and useful piece of American slang about people "who can dish it out and can take it." Now the people of this island can undoubtedly "dish it out," and I mean by that they have a very good opinion of themselves, tend to be self-complacent, and to patronise other people. But at the same time—by thunder!—"they can take it." When once they've made up their minds that sacrifices should be made, they'll make them. I believe I'm right in declaring that so long as they see the issue clearly and know they are being properly led, people here will impoverish themselves and face bankruptcy, if necessary, to challenge and combat the world-menace of Nazism.

As a further proof of this public determination I not only instance this dissatisfaction with the new budget but can add to that the fact that schemes of wartime finance and taxation that are downright revolutionary are already being welcomed. For example, it has been proposed that the whole procedure should be reversed, that instead of people receiving full payment for what they do and then giving a proportion of it to the government, it might be better if the government first took the lot and then returned to each citizen a proportion of his earnings. On this system there would be so much for each person for necessary expenses—and included in these might be actual rations of food—and then about a third of what a man earned would be returned to him. There is much to be said in favour of some such drastic scheme, first because it simplifies everything—and most of us want to get on with our work and don't want to be wasting time and energy filling up forms and arguing with the income-tax officials—and then it does relieve the formerly well-to-do people from the worry of trying to cope with previous commitments. To be personal for a moment, before this war I made a good deal of money out of my books and plays, especially the plays, which were often being done in several different countries at the same time. All that has gone, but on the other hand all the various commitments a man has on his hands when he's doing pretty well and feels he should share his luck still exist, and I still have a large family to educate, with the result that one has to live on dwindling savings. That doesn't matter. I don't think any of us are bothering much about money, these days. I can't myself believe that the old *laissez-faire* financial system can outlast this war either in this island or anywhere in Europe. But it would be much better to stop pretending that it is still in operation. That is probably at the root of the wide dissatisfaction with this new budget. So long as they are made to feel that we are all in the same boat and that every man and woman in that boat is pulling his or her weight, people here are

[131]

ready—nay, eager—to make every possible self-sacrifice, financial or otherwise.

I am glad to learn, from little quotations that come our way from the press across the Atlantic, that American journalists no longer consider that all is over with Great Britain, that there is now some faint hope that we may stagger along a few more months at least. Why they should ever have thought anything else is a mystery to me, and I sometimes wonder why German bounce and brag are so often accepted at their face value when the careful understatements of the British service people are so often misunderstood. Have you ever noticed that when the Nazis announce what they are going to do this island, it is assumed both by them and by many journalists who repeat their boasts that we here are not going to do anything at all by way of a reply. They talk almost as if this island were empty. They are going to mount big guns opposite Dover and Folkestone. They are going to assemble hundreds and hundreds of flat-bottomed troop-carrying barges. They are preparing an armada of troop-carrying planes. And so with this and that and the other, it will all be easy. And what are we supposed to be doing? Playing cricket, I suppose. Really one becomes very impatient with this childish stuff, which all has its root in a deliberate Nazi propaganda campaign. We have been facing the facts for some time here now.

XXI. Three Typical Factories
That Are Replying to Hitler

July 30, 1940

O NE OF the chief items of news here today is from the industrial front. The hours in the war factories are to be drastically reduced. The reason for that is that it would be impossible, without serious loss of health and output, to keep up the working hours of the last three months, when we made a terrific spurt to make up our deficiencies. Millions of workers here have been doing a seven-day, seventy- to eighty-hour week, which meant a tremendous strain. They have been giving some of these workers entertainments during their noonday break, but it was clear that what was needed was a reduction of hours to something like fifty-six a week, which will be quite sufficient to keep our war production up to full pitch once more workers have been trained. Already, hundreds of thousands of new workers—largely recruited from the unemployed, the black-coated class, and women—have been or are being trained by the government for this special wartime production. With the massive and energetic Mr. Bevin driving it on, the industrial front is hard at it, and so far its production has not been seriously interrupted by air raids.

What are these war factories like? I've seen a good

many of them in various parts of the country, of which three are typical. In the first factory, run by the government, they were making time fuses for anti-aircraft shells. These shells have a mechanism that can be set to allow for the time it takes the shell to reach the required height, and this mechanism has to be small, intricately exact, and strong enough to withstand the shock of its upward journey. The secret of the mass manufacture of this time-fuse mechanism is found, of course, in the use of machine tools. Ours is the machine-tool age, and the sooner we realise that fact and organise our political and economic life accordingly, the better it will be for us. I imagine that this time-fuse factory, with its keen youngish engineers and little army of girls in dark green overalls, could easily be switched over, in peace time, to the mass production of cheap but reliable watches and small clocks. It was a clean, neat, rather ladylike factory. There were hundreds and hundreds of machines buzzing away, but they were all clean, neat, tiny machines. As we walked through one long shed after another, these machines seemed to become steadily smaller and neater. And so it was with the parts they were turning out. The giant parts were only about an inch across. Before we had done I was being shown parts I could hardly see, no larger than half a very small pin. You couldn't believe it mattered whether they were there or not. All these midget bits and pieces have to be assembled, and when I realised this I stared with a new respect at the young superintendent who

[134]

was showing me round, for I'm certain that if I'd been left in charge of this fantastic job I'd have given it up when I looked at those miniature springs and screws and pins. But he only kept on apologising, telling me there was nothing spectacular here, just a rather difficult fiddling sort of job. I told him more than once that I was fascinated by his factory, with its miles of everything getting smaller and smaller, a kind of Snow White and the Seven Dwarfs munitions work, or—rather—Seven Dwarfs and thousands of Snow Whites. One of them was a spectacled and studious-looking girl, who might have been pressing wild flowers in a volume of sentimental verse; but actually the little machine she bent over was presenting her, all with an awful regularity and rapidity, with beautifully turned, tiny pieces of metal, and these, it appeared, were the strikers, which somewhere in distant mid-air would be released to detonate the shells. And then perhaps, because of one of these strikers and one of these shells, another girl far away, perhaps spectacled and studious-looking and sentimental like this one, wouldn't be able to see properly the machine she might be bending over, because the shell had done its work, a young life had gone, and she would be suddenly blind with tears and despair. All of which comes of imagining that because you have machine tools you no longer need God.

The second factory made gas masks, which are highly scientific contraptions that we need because we've decided to live in a hell-upon-earth. Our grandfathers could never have turned out these millions of gas masks. But to give them their due, our grandfathers—as we know from War Office records—indignantly refused to make any use of poison gas. Now, in these later and more ingenious days, the ends of the earth contribute to protect our children's lungs from the foul dews of our madness. The charcoal in the mask, which absorbs the gas, is manufactured from cocoanut shell from the West and East Indies, where no doubt thousands of people, with not a gas mask between them, idly wonder why we have such a passion for their cocoanut shells. The fine merino wadding, which is there to resist the particles in smoke clouds, comes from the great sheep farms of Australia. So when we put on our gas masks we are immediately in touch with the romantic tropics and the Antipodes. In this factory, I saw hundreds and hundreds of women and girls sitting in rows in a gigantic shed. Everything in there except the roof and the floor semed to be on the move. Along and above the tables were moving belts and travelling conveyors, and with these the women and girls had to keep time. They were really part of the machinery. If it was speeded up a notch or two, then they'd have to speed up a notch or two. Some of them worked so fast they seemed to have a dozen pairs of hands, like Indian goddesses. Some of them, who see that the charcoal is tamped down, have to count twenty all day long on their tamping machines, and I heard that in the street cars going home they still find themselves counting their twenties. Others would take a tin from the belt, put it under a machine for half a second, and then return it in a flash to another division of the belt. The tempo of the place was frightening. Hour after hour, morning till night, the belts and conveyors go humming along, the women's fingers flash right and left, and tin, charcoal, merino, metal springs and enamel are magically turned into gas-mask containers. And there is nothing free-and-easy about this rapid production, for all quantities are carefully weighed and all measurements accurately tested. Yet they were turning them out by the million. I'll confess that this kind of place is my idea of hell. But truth compels me to add that those women and girls didn't seem to mind it at all. The point is, women don't really associate themselves with these tasks; they are *in* but not *of* the machine; their fingers are hard at it but their minds are elsewhere, brooding over a sister's marriage or the young man who lodges farther down the street. Some of them were singing, loud and cheerfully. There mightn't seem much left to sing about in a world that kept you from morning till night making gas masks, but we are a brave as well as an idiotic species, and they sang away and seemed as happy as larks.

The third factory, which made aircraft, was more spectacular. The managing director, whom I found in an office that might have been in a Hollywood film set, explained what kind of aircraft his factory turned out, and then said I might as well have a preliminary view

of the main shed before his assistant manager showed
me over the whole works. So we walked along a corridor that reminded me of an alleyway in a big liner,
and at the end there was a doorway into a glass-
enclosed balcony. He said casually that this was it. And
it was: it was IT. I seemed to be looking down upon
a misty and twinkling great river of industry. You
couldn't call it a shed, it was a little town, all under
one roof and lit by thousands of greenish white lights.
In this unearthly illumination, like that of some other
kind of planet, I could see thousands of men below,
busy as ants. This was the middle of the morning, but
at any hour of the day and night it would have looked
just the same, for this factory worked twenty-four hours
a day, seven days a week. At one end of this giant shed,
so far away that through the glass of the balcony it
looked lost in greenish mist, the raw material of aircraft
manufacture arrives. At the other end, equally lost in
mist, were greeny-brown winged shapes, as if there were
a kind of termitary and the termites at that end had
achieved wings. Yes, raw material at one end, and airplanes coming out of the other. Afterwards I went
down to the floor of the shed and wandered through
a pandemonium of huge power presses, cutting out and
punching the metal, and batteries of drilling, milling,
slotting, shaping machines. In one wired-in section,
which looked comparatively negligible, I was told there
were seven hundred and fifty thousand pounds' worth
of machine tools. In the middle of this unbelievable

[138]

workshop was the standards room, which is insulated by rubber from the rest of the shed, and is sound-proof, dust-proof, air-conditioned at a constant sixty-eight degrees, and lit with artificial daylight from a combination of neon tubes. Here are kept the standards of measurement, down to half a ten-thousandth of an inch.

They were as thorough at sightseeing in that factory as they were at anything else. I wearied long before my guide did. The works are half a mile long and quarter of a mile wide. (And we have some bigger than this.) There was a paint or "dope" shop, as they call it, with a floor area of sixty thousand feet, and an enormous paint-mixing plant from which went five miles of copper paint pipes. There were nice little canteens, in which about five thousand persons could be served at a sitting . . . just homely little eating places. The army of folk in this factory wear between them forty different kinds of overalls, twelve types for women, twenty-eight for men, so that you can tell at a glance, once you know your forty varieties, who's who and doing what. They explained all this, and a thousand other things, to me, until my mind was as dizzy as my legs were tired. There's a point past which I can't take anything in, and I reached it in that aircraft factory.

This vast organisation wasn't a development extending over years of trial and error, but almost a rapid improvisation. Two years ago, they hadn't even cut the turf on this ground. It was all done, as we usually do things, hastily at the last minute. We didn't want to put up factories half a mile long, employing thousands and thousands of people working day and night, to build fighting airplanes. We'd much rather be building something else. That factory, like its fellow giants, came into existence because of Hitler and Goering, screaming about their air force and how they would bomb hell out of anybody who so much as contradicted them. Hitler and Goering and all their crazy young men are responsible for all this feverish activity. Those greeny-brown winged shapes at the far end of that unbelievable shed are going out to say a word or two, by way of reply, for democracy.

XXII. Reply to Mr. Glens Falls, New York

August 5, 1940

I wish I could answer all the splendid letters I am receiving, by every mail, from all the Dominions, from Central and South America, and from all parts of the United States. They are both welcome and useful. But there is one I particularly want to answer, not because it is very friendly and welcome—because it isn't— but because it represents a point of view that needs examining. As I have no permission to give the writer's name, I'll merely say that this letter arrived yesterday, and that it comes from Glens Falls, New York State. And I propose to deal with this letter, which expresses the pure isolationist point of view, in the friendliest but frankest possible manner.

The writer begins by saying, "Let's be honest with each other." Well, that suits me. I've been called many things—conceited, bumptious, domineering, tactless— but never dishonest and deceitful. Then, after asking us to be honest with each other, the writer goes on to say, "Great Britain, under the guise of a holy hypocrisy, the equal of which has been approached only by America, fights only for the preservation of the status quo of the British Empire which is a perfectly legitimate goal as the world goes. Just a few years ago we saved and materially enlarged that Empire—and paid the whole bill. Now we are being called to the rescue again."

[141]

Let's deal with that paragraph, point by point. In the first place, where is this "guise of holy hypocrisy" he talks about? Great Britain is fighting to rescue Europe to-day, and the rest of the world tomorrow, from the domination of a gang of liars, looters and murderers, who wherever they have gone so far have destroyed human liberty and all possibility of real progress. If Glens Falls does not recognise these facts, then Glens Falls is both blind and deaf. In this fight for elementary liberties, Britain has been joined by the great dominions of the Empire out of their own free choice. One member of this commonwealth, Eire, has decided for neutrality, to the danger of both herself and Britain. But we recognise that this is her affair. As for the "status quo" of the British Empire or anything else, this kind of talk is twenty-five years out of date. Everything now is rushing into the melting-pot, and we are fighting to see that something good and not something evil comes out of that pot in the end. Again, in the last war, America did not "pay the whole bill." At the end of the war America found herself with a mass of war debts owing to her. But then so did Great Britain. We also found ourselves saddled with a greater loss still, namely, one million dead. We have not recovered from this loss yet. The paragraph ends: "We are being called to the rescue again". But it is not a question of anybody being called to the rescue. What we here have been content to do, and we have done it very modestly, with less vehemence than many well-known American commentators, is to call the attention of the American people to the facts. What these are we shall see when we deal with the next paragraph of this letter.

The writer goes on to say: "But we have learned a lot of things, not the least of which is that if Mother Britannia and Grandmother Germania can't live together peacefully in the old family homestead, it is stark tragedy, of course, but it is no justification for the subtle suggestion that Son Sammy commit hara-kiri in that continually recurring struggle for empire."

Now let's examine this example of out-of-date and dangerous thinking. And don't let's make any mistake that it *is* out-of-date and dangerous. It is just the sort of stuff that Goebbels and his agents want pushed about, because they know how untrue—but also how useful to them—it is. To begin with, there isn't an old family homestead called Europe, there is only the old family homestead of the whole wide world. And let me give our friend one example of how interdependent we are in this world. In October 1929 there was a sudden crisis in Wall Street, when stocks went rocketing down instead of up, and this was followed by a vast slump, the effect of which was soon felt in Europe. Germany's export trade was cut down by 35 per cent. Her unemployment figures soared to unprecedented heights, with the immediate result that the Nazi Party, which had made little or no headway for years and was not taken seriously, suddenly had an enormous influx of recruits and supporters, and in the election of July 1932 polled more than any other party, though at no time had it a clear majority over all other parties. The present war is entirely the creation of the power-crazy Nazi Party. That party would never have been more than a minor movement if the German unemployment figures had not suddenly jumped to such a height. Those figures were the result of a world economic slump. And the beginning of that slump in my opinion can be traced to the record selling of nearly 20 million shares on the 23rd of October, 1929, on Wall Street.

So much for Mother Britannia and Grandmother Germania bickering in the old family homestead. Moreover, during the years immediately before the outbreak of this war, the efforts of the British Government to come to some kind of peaceful understanding with the Nazis were so strenuous and were made with such a sacrifice of British prestige that nearly every newspaper in America was howling that Britain was decadent and afraid to fight for democracy. Whether the policy of our ministers was right or wrong is another question, but obviously nobody has any justification for jeering at them all over again because they will fight. Again it was during these same years that the biggest network of Nazi intrigue and espionage, involving a great expenditure of money and an elaborate organisation, was discovered not in the old family homestead of Europe but in the United States, to which the Nazis were giving more and more of their attention, just as they had been sending more and more of their agents to various countries in South America. Does this suggest a purely European quarrel? It does not. These facts prove that the Nazi plan is a plan for world domination or nothing. To assume anything else is to do exactly what Britain was accused of doing a year or two ago, namely, sticking your head in the sand and pretending you can't see any danger. One whole group of newspapers here used to give us these very same arguments, telling us to isolate ourselves, that these quarrels that began in Central Europe were no concern of ours, that we must turn our faces towards our own Empire and—apparently—pretend that the continent of Europe didn't exist. The absurdity of these arguments is so obvious now that these newspapers pretend they've never heard of them. They are a wilful ignoring of the facts. You are, my dear sir, years and years and years out-of-date. You are trying to live in the last century, not in this. These pictures of Mother Britannia and Grandmother Germania in the old family homestead simply don't represent reality any longer. They're merely an excuse for not thinking properly and not taking necessary action. You don't want to be involved in war. Of course you don't. But then neither do we, we who disarmed so thoroughly that now our men—yes, and girls too—have had to work at their machines from morning till night for seven days a week until they were ready to drop. The harmless folk in Poland, Norway, Holland, Belgium didn't want war either, but they found themselves, one terrible morning, being bombed and machine-gunned without mercy. And why? Because dear old Grandmother Germania had built up a vast war machine that she was determined to use, either as blackmail, to frighten other people into accepting a complete loss of freedom, or as a weapon to batter her way to world domination. And when I say world domination, I mean it—the real thing, the old Genghis Khan stuff, you do the work while they crack the whip. This Grandmother Germania you talk of isn't the granny you have in mind at all. It's the false granny from the Red Riding Hood tale, the wolf who's put on the old woman's nightdress and spectacles. No doubt that in Glens Falls it all seems a long way off, but that's no excuse for talking nonsense about it. And really it isn't a long way off. It would have been in the last century, but we're living in an age when lightning communications and super-fast transport have considerably reduced the size of the world. It used to take Sir Walter Scott about a week to travel from Edinburgh to London. The same journey's been done lately in about an hour. That's the kind of world it is, whether for better or worse, and whether it is for better or worse depends a good deal on what happens in this present conflict.

And now for your final remarks, in which you say "America can conserve and develop her spiritual, material and intellectual resources behind her own impregnable ramparts—and thus become, like Byzantium of old, the rallying point for defeated humanity—the

Citadel of a New Rome." Let's have a look at this fine flourish.

The fact is, you haven't impregnable ramparts. The only impregnable ramparts that the Nazis would recognise are vast navies, air forces and armies, and at the moment you haven't got them. True, you propose to build them, but it's going to take several years at the earliest, and before then one of two things will have happened. Either we shall have broken the Nazis, in which case you won't want those arms on which you're prepared to spend so much. Or—the Nazis will have broken us, in which case they will attack you long before you are ready for them. You may ask, Why should they attack you? The answer is easy. First, because the conflict with us will have brought them very near you; secondly, they don't like you any more than they like us; thirdly, knowing their mentality, I assure you that, flushed and half-crazy with victory, they will want to keep the vast military machine turning over and gathering more loot.

As for conserving and developing material and spiritual resources, you cannot make the most of your material resources isolated from the rest of the world, as your traders are discovering already. Good trade needs a confident, peaceful world, and you haven't got it. Your spiritual resources are your own affair, but I take leave to doubt if a pretended indifference to one of the profoundest conflicts in the history of man is going to make a good basis for the development of spiritual resources. And for my part, I don't want to see America becoming like Byzantium, but behaving like America, where men went to become free and equal, where democracy and liberty, for which we are fighting, found its great home.

And that, dear Mr. Glens Falls, is my reply.

XXIII. Grand Man of the People

August 6, 1940

I HAD A long talk yesterday with the greatest new personality and force in the British Government—that is, the Minister of Labour and National Service, Ernest Bevin. Now I'll confess to you that it has long been my opinion that politicians as a class are very much over-rated in this country, so that when I meet any man in political life—if I may be Irish for a moment—I always expect to be disappointed. Like the old Scots woman who was told in the kirk that faith could move mountains, so went home and prayed that a mountain at the back of her cottage should be removed, but when she got up next morning and saw it still there, she muttered, "Ay, Ah thocht as much." Well, usually after I've just met some political figure for the first time, I go home muttering, "Ay, I thought as much." But not after talking to Ernest Bevin.

Here's a man after my own heart. He's a Bristol man, in his sixties now, and for years has been the general secretary of the Transport Workers Union. He's been taught in a hard school. He's a massively built man, with a face of great breadth and character, and darkish twinkling eyes, for he's a man with any amount of humour and devilment in him. He's a fighter and he's a sound organiser, but to me what chiefly distinguishes him from most of his colleagues is not only depth of character but a rare sagacity, the product of years of valuable experience working on a naturally shrewd mind. It's that kind of sagacity that you can't get merely by having been expensively educated, by listening to a lot of lectures or reading thousands of books. It comes from first-hand experience. And it belongs to the people. Old farmers and horse-dealers and fishermen often acquire it. About a great many Left Wing personages there's a sort of thinness and brittleness, a flavourless cardboard quality. Though they may denounce all academies, nevertheless they themselves are academic. But Bevin seems to me one of those rare leaders of the people—and probably the finest example of them is Lincoln—who have somehow accumulated in themselves that shrewdness, that deep sagacity, that rich humanity which can be distilled from the experience of the people. And in ten weeks—weeks of prodigious reorganising—Bevin has made himself the greatest force in the country, apart of course from the Prime Minister himself. These two men—Winston Churchill and Ernest Bevin—come from the opposite ends of English society, and would seem to have little or nothing in common, but actually they work well together and respect each other for the fine rich lumps of English character that they are.

In taking over the Ministry of Labour and National Service, Bevin took on a terrific job. Its importance can't be exaggerated. It was partly what were called the "bottle-necks"—that is, the hold ups—in our supply of skilled labour that made our initial output of munitions so disappointing. Bevin came in at a time when it was absolutely imperative that there should be a colossal drive in production such as Great Britain has never known before. And the whole problem bristled with appalling difficulties and snags. We are a democratic people, and refuse to be herded about like sheep or treated like serfs, like the people in the totalitarian states. We had to make this prodigious effort, and yet at the same time we had to preserve those liberties for which we are fighting. No man in the country was more aware of these problems than the new Minister of Labour, who had been fighting for his trade unions for thirty or forty years and yet at the same time knew full well that Nazism had to be destroyed. (It was Bevin who pointed out that in all the terrible story of fifth columns and corruption from Norway down to France, no working folk or organisation of workers could be found prominently figuring.) So this massive man went tearing into his terrific job, scattering timid officials right and left, but at the same time preserving that easy deep sagacity. And don't imagine that what he accomplished— and is still creating—is no concern of anybody outside this island, for some of these problems are really world problems, involving as they do the relations between authority, governmental and industrial, and the workers themselves. In these matters Britain, even at this crisis, is acting again as a sort of political and economic laboratory for the modern world. I know that we often appear an old-fashioned folk, overfond of tradition, but this side of the national medal is exhibited too often, so that many people overseas forget the other side, showing us as a people with a highly developed system of social services and industrial relations. Bevin had to find, at once, the maximum output from our war industries with the minimum interference with our liberties.

The result was his Conditions of Employment and National Arbitration Order 1940, an order made under the Defence Regulations. This retains and requires the full use of voluntary joint arrangements for the settlement of trade disputes, relating to hours of work, pay, conditions, etc.—making full use of the joint councils of employers and workers already in existence; but it also sets up a National Arbitration Tribunal to which trade disputes, reported to the Minister and not settled by the Joint Councils, will be referred. Strikes and lockouts are prohibited unless the dispute has been reported to the Minister and twenty-one days have elapsed without the dispute having been settled by the National Tribunal. This order also requires the observance of all employers of terms and conditions of employment not less favourable than what are called "recognised terms and conditions," which are those settled by previous negotiations between employers and trade unions. The National Arbitration Tribunal consists of five members, three of them appointed members, not representing either side, and the other two members selected from panels of employers' and workers' representatives.

If all this seems pretty dull stuff, I apologise, but actually it is not. It represents a genuine working system of what Mr. Bevin himself calls Industrial Democratic Control, and when you consider that it has been set in motion during the gravest national crisis in the history of this country, with an immediate threat of invasion over our heads, it is a triumph of sensible corporate living, containing an immense promise for the future. But that is not all. It is, in fact, only the beginning. Although this country is now engaged in making the most colossal war effort ever known in history—for it must be remembered that Nazi Germany's similar effort extended over years, and was built up with a ruthless disregard for the rights of the individual—our social services have not only not been curtailed but in many fields have actually been increased and enlarged. We are not doing less for the people than we were doing, but are doing more. For example, unemployment assistance and insurance—and though unemployment has been immensely reduced, this rapid shift from peacetime to wartime conditions cannot take everybody in at once—have been increased in rates and benefits. The age limit for Old Age and Widows' Pensions has been reduced and supplementary pensions have been added. The minimum of agricultural wages has been recently raised. The Superannuation Schemes Act of 1940 has been passed to prevent any loss of rights under any superannuation scheme that might otherwise result from employees going into the armed forces or into civil employment for war purposes. Then the Minister of Labour has established, and acts as chairman of, a Factory and Welfare Advisory Board, which assists in stimulating and developing to the fullest possible extent the health, safety and welfare arrangements inside the factories, and the billeting, communal feeding and welfare arrangements outside the factory. Inside the factories, this scheme co-operates with employers to ensure the safety, health and well-being of the workers, the provision of medical, nursing and welfare services, and to reduce the risk of breakdown or overstrain. Experts have been called in to give advice about hours of work, the necessary rest pauses, the general conditions of working, and the providing of food and drink in the factory canteens. There are even entertainments for workpeople in the big war factories at meal times or rest pauses, which are being run by the organisation known as E.N.S.A. from its initials, which was started to provide entertainment for the armed forces.

So much for welfare inside the factory. Outside the factory, these welfare schemes don't work with employers because Bevin, as he told me yesterday, wishes to avoid any suspicion of setting up or encouraging what he calls "industrial feudalism," that system in which the employer takes a too paternal interest in the leisure of his workers, as if he were responsible for their whole existence and they had no life apart from him, a dangerously undemocratic system. So the Ministry has appointed divisional and local welfare officers, who are attached to local labour supply committees, and act in co-operation with the local authorities and the various voluntary organisations, which may be dealing with anything from pigeon-breeding to the higher drama, from football to sonatas. The job of these officers is not to impose their idea of suitable recreation on the workers, but to see that wartime conditions are not allowed to squeeze these voluntary recreational organisations out of existence, that there's a chance both for the chap who likes a bit of sport and the fellow who'd like to act or play the fiddle. This welfare work is further complicated by the fact that workers, often after being trained by the government, are now frequently transferred to new areas—for the whole industrial map of Britain is rapidly being changed, and at the end of this war we shan't know the place—and this movement means elaborate arrangements for travelling and lodging allowances, as well as more systematic welfare work for the more remote areas.

This is just a glimpse of what this new Ministry of Labour and National Service is doing, with the tremendous drive of its massive and great-hearted minister behind it. But I think that Bevin's latest project is perhaps the one nearest his heart, if only because, years ago, it was he who organised the International Transport Workers, whose influence is not dead today even at this time of universal mistrust and misunderstanding.

This latest project is the organisation of international labour in this country, for we have Polish, Norwegian, Czech, Dutch, Belgian, French soldiers, sailors and airmen ready to fight for us here. It is Bevin's great scheme to build up, behind these new foreign legions, an army of international workers hard at it helping to turn out the munitions of war for their fellow-countrymen and for the embattled democracies.

This then is what this grand man of the people is doing.

XXIV. The Nazi Propaganda Machine Must Wobble Badly

August 8, 1940

WE USUALLY credit the Nazis with considerable—even diabolical—skill in making propaganda, but lately I have been wondering if this propaganda of theirs isn't more remarkable for quantity than for quality. Consider the present situation. They have told us for the last six weeks that they are about to invade us at any moment, and we have made our preparations accordingly. Those preparations, as everybody who knows anything about them will agree, are both extensive and thorough. Again, as everybody agrees, the spirit of our people here is very high. The war of nerves isn't being won by the Germans, as any student of human nature could have told them it wouldn't be, for apprehensiveness and nervousness are not weaknesses of the British, who tend always to be too self-confident and complacent. The Germans, though courageous enough, are a more nervous people than we are. And it looks as if this long war of nerves has had more effect in Berlin than in London.

I don't say this because I know what's happening in Berlin. I haven't the least idea what's happening there. But I know what's happening in London, and that is, something very different from the fantastic stories that appear in the German radio and press. When people are reduced to broadcasting and printing solemnly this sort of drivel, their propaganda machine must be beginning to wobble badly.

For example, what is one to make of nonsense like this? "Londoners," said the Nazi radio at Zeesen, "are now so panic-stricken that they are drunk every night. Alcoholic poisoning has increased by leaps and bounds of late." But Zeesen can do better than that, and did, on the 17th of July, when it announced that "Crowds gather from the early morning before the premises of London astrologers to gain information as to England's fate." But *Deutschlandsender* went one better than this on the very same day, when it said that London cinemas are losing their audiences because "No one feels like going to the cinema any more since they must always expect that at any moment the lights may go up and a demand be made for volunteers to dig trenches in the streets of London."

We are also told that we have nothing to eat but horse-flesh, that tea is two pounds sterling per pound, that the streets of London are given up to orgies and dancing, that rich English ladies are marrying foreign dock workers to secure foreign nationality, that when a gas main exploded in Plumstead, Piccadilly (which incidentally is miles away) became in a few minutes like a madhouse. And so it goes on. They'll be announcing soon that, so terrible is our despair, that Mickey Mouse and Donald Duck have been appointed respectively to command the army and navy.

I say that people who have to put out such drivel, which is an insult to the intelligence of the people who listen to or read it, must be worrying about what they can tell their audiences. Apparently the German public is ready to swallow any rubbish, so long as it will keep them away from reality for an hour or two. This is the only explanation of the bombastic stuff that Nazi generals are putting on the air, telling everybody how easy it is for them to conquer this island and how terrible it will be for us. But why keep on boasting about it? Why not get on with it? If they think they're frightening us, they're sadly mistaken. But perhaps they make these loud threatening noises all the time to keep up their own courage and confidence. A General Sander, of the German Air Force, has been telling German listeners what his bombers are going to do to us, how the attack will be made in continuous waves, how they are all ready to strike, and the rest of it. As the *Times* says: "In the whole of his talk the General seems to have overlooked one point—namely that Britain possesses a service known as the Royal Air Force, and that that Force has already shown itself capable of taking on anything that the Luftwaffe can send here. . . ."

Exactly. If one body of men has caught the imagination of the world so far in this war it is the men of the Royal Air Force, who time after time have shown themselves superior in skill, initiative and dash to the much-vaunted German Luftwaffe. In France these men fought against the most appalling odds, hurling their fighters against the massed ranks of German bombers until they could hardly see from weariness, finally establishing a local superiority above Dunkirk that the full weight of the German Air Force could not break. It would be difficult to overpraise these young men, though I must say that our Air Ministry can hardly be accused of trying it, and it's a pity that a tradition of quiet modesty, admirable though it may be in itself, has been carried so far that many of the more spectacular performances of these modern knights errant are never given the world.

XXV. A Few Words to the Pot-and-
Kettle Theorists

August 11, 1940

I WANT TO examine a certain attitude of mind towards this war that is to me the most maddening of all, and this attitude of mind is the pot and kettle—or six of one and half a dozen of the other. People who think like this always have a very knowing, cynical, behind-the-scenes, let-me-give-you-the-low-down air about them. You can't take them in. No pulling the wool over *their* eyes. As a matter of fact, these people are manipulated by Nazi propaganda as if they were sheep being herded. For if the Nazis can't get outsiders to feel that they are the saviours of the world, and this takes a bit of doing even by liars as ambitious and fluent as the Goebbels troop, then the next best thing is to persuade all the simpletons in neutral countries that there is nothing to choose between the sides in this conflict. It's as if several decent citizens were set upon by some gangsters, who called out to passers-by not to take any notice because this is a very tough neighbourhood and they often had little quarrels of this sort. The more innocent of these passers-by would shake their heads and move on, murmuring what a pity it was that men couldn't find more profitable and civilised methods of spending their time. All of which would be very bad luck on those decent citizens, who would find themselves not only refused assistance but also insulted into the bargain. The only persons who would gain would be the gangsters. The pot-and-kettle trick would have worked.

Now the Nazis are always working this trick. Probably the best example is their relation to the small neutral states of Western Europe. As we all know, as soon as Germany decided it would pay her to invade these states, she marched into them, as she did into Norway, Denmark, Holland, Belgium. Her excuse always was that she was forestalling Britain, who was just about to do the same thing herself. A few weeks after the Gestapo had got going in these countries, documents were always found *proving* that everything had been set for their invasion by Britain. These are all lies just as the documents are, of course, blatant forgeries. Nobody outside Germany—for inside Germany there's a capacity for swallowing nonsense that is simply fabulous—entirely believes this tricky stuff, but what happens is that the pot-and-kettle people are vaguely confirmed in their opinion and feel that Britain and Germany are equally unscrupulous but that Germany is the smarter and quicker rogue. In short, the trick has worked.

Let me give you another and more typical example. Goebbels seems to have decided that all British recent losses in the air and at sea should roughly be multiplied by ten. Thus, if a hundred thousand tons of shipping have been sunk, call it a round million. If five British fighters have been brought down, call it fifty. There is a cheerful impudence about this that almost commands my admiration. But anybody far from the scene of fighting may say, "You tell us that these losses are multiplied by ten, but how do we know that the Nazi claims aren't really accurate?" To that I would reply: First, what is the attitude of the Nazis towards bold and impudent lying? Do they dislike it and try to avoid it at all costs? On the contrary, they admit, following their master Adolf, that there is much to be gained by telling lies, especially if they are thumping big lies. Therefore it is likely they are putting out thumping big lies now. Secondly, it is quite possible for anybody anywhere, no matter how far from the actual fighting, to prove that the Nazis and the Fascists have put out the grossest and most impudent fictions. For example, if all their claims for the sinking of our capital warships are added up, the grand total comes to far more capital ships than we possess. Not only have they sunk *all* our battleships, big cruisers and aircraft carriers, but they have apparently gone on to sink similar great ships that we haven't even built yet. In the same way, if you accepted all their figures for the tonnage of commercial shipping that has been sunk, you would discover that we had practically no shipping left, yet on top of that they go and sink another *million tons* in the last three weeks. No doubt this month they will claim to have sunk two million tons, and I see no reason why, before the year is out, they shouldn't be claiming to have sent to the bottom ten or twenty million tons a month.

Now the absurdity of this is obvious. But the pot-and-kettle man says: "Yes, I know the Nazis tell a lot of lies, but then that's part of the game, and the British are playing the same game, so they tell a lot of lies too, and it's all propaganda and you can't believe anybody." And he doesn't realise that as soon as he's said this, though Goebbels may have missed him with the first barrel of his gun, Goebbels has hit him squarely with the second barrel. Because it simply isn't true that both parties are playing the same game. One party, the Nazis, believe in telling thumping big lies. The other party, ourselves, are only anxious to give the world the exact truth. If the Air Ministry here announces that sixty German planes have been brought down, you may depend upon it that exactly sixty German planes have been seen to crash, and that a great deal of trouble has been taken to make the figure as accurate as is humanly possible. Similarly, if the Admiralty says that two ships of a combined tonnage of 2,540 tons have been sunk, then that is the tonnage, and not the fantastic figure the Nazis claim.

Many of my friends in the United States have written to me saying how much more efficient Nazi propaganda has been in the States than ours has been. Obviously they imagine that there are two large propaganda machines hard at work in the United States, one run by the Nazis, the other run by Britain, and that the Nazi is the better machine. But the fact is, there aren't two propaganda machines working in the United States, there is only one, the Nazi. It is not that we have a similar organisation there that is less efficient, we simply have no such organisation, so that my friends are criticising the working of something that doesn't exist. There aren't two sets of propaganda experts, backed by millions of money, getting at the pot-and-kettle folk in the United States—there is only one set, the Nazis. I remember these same friends used to warn me that whereas the Nazis were flooding the newspapers and periodicals of the States with fine photographs, we were doing little or nothing, and that this was very bad for us. My reply to that used to be that, although it would be very nice to have more photographs of our war effort circulated throughout the United States, we people here felt we were engaged in a life-and-death struggle for democracy and freedom everywhere, that the issue was fundamentally a moral one, and that spectators of such a desperate conflict who depended on photographs to make up their minds for them hardly seemed worth influencing at all. Such people, I added, if they saw a man battling with a tiger, would apparently side with the tiger if it sent out the better photographs of itself. But of course the pot-and-kettle cynics will retort that this is not a case of a man battling with a tiger, but of two sets of fallible human beings opposed to each other. They will also say that we people may talk grandly about moral issues, but that the fact remains that what we are fighting for is to keep what we've got.

I think this last charge is worth a careful examination. In the first place I deny that our war aims are merely the restoration of the world to what it was, let us say, ten years ago, before Hitler rose to power and began charging about Europe. Let me add this from my own personal experience. In my forty-five years I have never heard or come into contact with more discussions and correspondence attempting to plan a new world order than I have done during these past three months, in spite of the fact that during this period we have been threatened with immediate invasion and have had to work day and night on our defences. The British people are not thinking about defending their island—though they're going to do that, all right—but they're also arguing, discussing, planning, generally fermenting. The most popular talks I've given on the air here have been those referring to the possibility of a new order of things. The Britain now fighting this war is very far removed from what some of us called "the weary rich old man" and attacked before this war. Britain is tremendously alive, and at this moment is probably the youngest nation on earth.

To say that there is no difference between these decent, hopeful, chivalrous folk and the gang that has invaded and looted half Western Europe, that alternates between bullying and whining and never speaks in a level reasonable voice, is to confess to a complete intellectual and moral bankruptcy, to admit that right and wrong no longer mean anything, that the world is a chaos and will rapidly be a hell. This isn't being well-informed and shrewd, it's being cowardly and idiotic. It's pretending in order to dodge responsibilities. I say that even if it were true, which it certainly isn't, that we had no war aims beyond keeping our own Empire intact and out of the hands of Nazis and Fascists, we still have a right to expect the sympathy of decent and sensible people everywhere. The British Empire is not going to be taken apart by Nazis and Fascists, but if it were, if it were suddenly discovered to be in the hands of the swaggering and scheming back-parlour gangsters of Central Europe, who would use every new possession as a base for further conquest, these cool pot-and-kettle theorists would wake up one morning to find that the decent pot had vanished and that the kettle was now steaming in their shrinking scalded faces. I wouldn't willingly hand over the worst fever-stricken little island we possess to such a gang. And that is my reply, my first and I hope my last, to the pot-and-kettle school of responsibility dodgers.

XXVI. A Tribute to the Real Heroes and Heroines of the War

August 22, 1940

I RETURNED last night from a little holiday. I needed a short rest, for I'd been working very hard without a break for months, and also I wanted to see my children, who'd been away at school. So we all had a holiday together among the mountains of Wales, where we did a lot of walking and scrambling and slipping. I went from London to these mountains by motor car, and then returned yesterday, by a different route altogether, by train. If you look at a map you'll see that I crossed almost the full middle width of this country, between five and six hundred miles, and that I passed through some of our most important industrial districts. Now I mention this because both going there and coming back I looked carefully for any signs of air-raid damage —for shattered factories, ruined houses, bomb craters along roads or in fields—and neither going there nor coming back did I see one single tiny piece of evidence that there had ever been an air raid. And this during the very time when the Nazis were boasting that they were bringing this country in ruins about our ears! I saw no sign of them or their works.

What I did see were boys playing cricket and football, girls playing tennis, soldiers doing physical drill, soldiers waiting for their girl friends, girls waiting for their soldier friends, people queueing up for the movies, the vast army of our munition workers going to and from their factories—and, once or twice, some restless specks in the sky, roaming hungrily in the blue, the terrible Spitfires, waiting to swoop down upon any invading squadron. My train came in exactly to time, and except that it was crowded with soldiers going on or returning from leave, I'd never have known from the behaviour of this train that we were at war at all. And that is the exact truth.

Probably there are some—though I hope and trust, not many—who will be disappointed because their blood isn't being curdled and their hair made to stand on end by some frightful description of bombs crashing and buildings tottering and bodies being dragged out of ruins and fountains of blood and tears. I don't propose to apologise because I'm not handing out such blood-curdling stuff. This is not a horror story, but a tribute, as warmly enthusiastic as I can make it, to the real heroes and heroines of this war so far, the people who stand out from this dark welter of cowardice, treachery and panic like a Gibraltar—and that is, the ordinary folk of Britain. Many weeks ago—it was when France was collapsing and many thought it was all up with us—I wrote that I pinned my faith on the ordinary folk of Britain, whom I think I know about as well as anybody knows them, and now everything that has happened since has gloriously justified and confirmed that faith.

It's probably a very good thing for us all that Hitler
and Mussolini are not men who have travelled very
far. They've neither of them been to Britain. They've
never met the ordinary British folk, never even caught
a glimpse of them at work or at play, and don't really
know—except at secondhand—what kind of people live
in this island. They've met ambassadors and the like,
but not the people. And that, in my opinion, is where—
and why—they've gone wrong. They ought to have
known—and if they'd read their history books carefully
and hadn't listened to agents who were busy making out
a case they would have known—that the English are a
rather sleepy, good-natured, complacent people, who
just don't want to bother doing anything very much—
until they're roused, but if once you thoroughly rouse
them, they'll work or fight till they drop. And that's just
what these dictators, with their threats and bogey-bogey
talk, have gone and done. With the result that as the
blitzkrieg has come nearer and nearer, the *morale* of
these people has gone up by leaps and bounds. Some
government departments may have made one or two
panicky moves, such as the wholesale interning of
refugees, many of whom would have been very useful
to us, but there hasn't been the slightest trace of panic
among the people themselves, and it's the people themselves, by the way, who've been quick to protest against
hasty and unjust official actions. Their courage is magnificently high. I don't know whether the house-maid
did announce demurely, "Please, madam—bombs!" or

whether the mother *did* say to her daughter, "Now put down that book and pay attention to the air raid," but that really is the spirit—a spirit not so much of bravado as of cool acceptance, a determination not to be panicky or even flustered, not to be, as they're fond of saying, "put out" by air raids or anything else. And I'm convinced it's a spirit that the dictators, who've lived for years now among people whose sense of independence has been completely crushed, simply don't understand. It's as if a man who'd been used to handling sheep suddenly found himself faced with a pack of lively fox terriers. The good old technique just won't work. If it's a question of a war of nerves, these people here will still be getting on with their lives as best they can when the German populace are half-crazy with apprehension.

If this sounds a brutal thing to say, I must point out that we didn't begin this war of nerves or war of anything else, that we showed ourselves willing to make almost any concession, to be jeered at and sneered at as being decadent, rather than plunge into this madness again; but the Nazis wanted and now they're getting it. And that's another thing about these people here, these ordinary English, Scots, Welsh—they've got exactly the right spirit about this war. They're not indulging in orgies of hate and blood-lust. They've kept every scrap of their usual sanity and decency. In some countries, enemy airmen who came over to bomb and machine-gun civilians, even children playing in the fields, and hap-

pened to fall among the people they were attacking
would be torn to pieces by infuriated mobs. But not here,
among these people. Wounded Nazi airmen have been as
carefully tended as if they were our own. Pilots who've
landed by parachute among us have been given ciga-
rettes and cups of tea. It's true that the other day one
of them wasn't so lucky, but he was one of those ill-
mannered sneering cubs that the Nazis have turned out
in such large numbers, and he jeered at the English
workman who told him to put his hands up, so the
workman promptly hit him on the nose. If they want
it rough, they can have it rough. But there's no hating
behind all this—none of that rather sadistic war fever
that sometimes seizes whole populations. In its place is
a solid determination to have done once and for all with
these power-crazy lunatics, who refuse to settle down
and get on with an ordinary decent life. If this war
machine of theirs simply can't stop, then we feel that
it'll have to be broken to bits, and the folk are ready to
go on hammering, if need be for years, until it *is* broken
to bits. That's the primary determination of the British
people, but although carrying it out means an immense
effort—and I doubt if any nation in the history of the
world ever made a bigger effort than we're making
now—no one must imagine that we too are content to
be nothing but cogs in a war machine. Not a bit of it.
The people everywhere here seem to me far more alive,
in every possible sense of that term, than they were a
year or so ago. They're not only ready to fight Hitler,

but they're eager for a better quality of life than they had before. They're awake and indeed on the march to a better way of living. You notice this all the time in half a hundred different ways.

Let me give one tiny example, from something I know personally. Some weeks ago I helped in an effort to save our great London Philharmonic Orchestra. Well, not only has that orchestra been saved, but at this present moment it's doing what no great symphony orchestra has ever done before here—it's touring the big vaudeville theatres in the provinces—while here in London the orchestra gives nightly concerts, the Proms, as they're called—and these concerts of good music in these vaudeville theatres are playing to packed houses. That's just one example of that fine stirring of life here, that awakening demand for a better quality of living, which accompanies, don't forget, the most stupendous sudden war effort any country's ever been called upon to make.

About eighteen months ago, I wrote a series of articles in a newspaper here called "Britain, Wake Up!" and they attracted a good deal of attention. And when I said "Britain, Wake Up," I meant it. The title wasn't just a journalist's stunt. I was beginning to feel depressed about this country. I felt its people were half-asleep, and that the smell of decay was in the air. It's that, of course, which deceived the Nazis and the Fascists, and led them to imagine they had only to pull frightful faces at us and we'd let them take our Empire to pieces. Now they know better. And I know better, for I shouldn't dream of saying "Britain, Wake Up!" now, for the people are not only wide awake but are growing visibly in mental and moral stature, and are proving themselves once more to be what I always knew in my heart they were—these decent, kindly, courageous, ordinary folk of Britain—namely, the salt of the earth. And not only to the magnificent young men who sweep the skies, but even to some nameless old man or woman found crushed among the ruins, you would apply Wordsworth's glorious lines:

> Thou hast left behind
> Powers that still work for thee; air, earth and skies;
> There's not a breathing of the common wind
> That will forget thee; thou hast great allies;
> Thy friends are exultations, agonies,
> And love, and man's unconquerable mind. . . .

XXVII. Air-Raid Life Is a
Queer Existence

August 27, 1940

A WORD of this air-raid life of ours. It's a queer existence. I'm not going to pretend I like it. To a very busy man it's exasperating because no matter how you contrive to make the best of these conditions— they *do* waste your time. Your programme of work and engagements, which may have been planned to a very careful time-table, is broken by these constant raids and warnings, and of course it's a nuisance. But we carry on.

Last night, for instance, I had arranged to see a film producer and his assistant at my house, to discuss an important film we're planning; and they arrived just after the alarm went, so instead of talking upstairs, we went downstairs into the basement and held our conference there, and except for occasional moments when the thudding of bombs seemed near and we gave each other a questioning glance, we simply got on with our job. I have no air-raid shelter in my house, and so we all pop down to the basement floor, which is just below ground level. This may not be as safe as an outside shelter but at least it has the advantage of being indoors, so that we haven't to go trooping out into the night. My neighbour is an air-raid warden, and has quite a large shelter in the garden, and some of the folk in the small houses across the way use this shelter, and immediately after the alarm has gone I hear them hurrying next door, carrying their babies. They have music and games down there, and do themselves proud.

Yesterday afternoon I looked in at the dress rehearsal of a play of mine that is being revived—it opened tonight—and I hadn't been ten minutes in the theatre before the sirens began wailing. "What do we do now?" I asked the manager. "Oh," he said, "we keep on until we hear bombs or gunfire very close, and then we break off and go down into the green room." There weren't any sounds of close bombs or gunfire, so they kept on, and showed no signs of being worried by the alarm. But then a dress rehearsal is such a desperate business to an actor that I suppose a mere air-raid alarm at the same time makes no difference.

I was very pleased with the story that came out of yesterday afternoon's alarm, which described how one of the men who sell little mechanical toys—and his toys were tiny walking men—somewhere along Oxford Street, found that when the alarm went and the crowds on the pavement melted away, he had for once all the space he wanted, even if he hadn't any prospective customers, so he set his mechanical little men walking about all over the pavement, and said to a passer-by, "I'm just giving the poor little beggars an outing." That's a true story, and I like it because its touch of humour and fancy is like a sudden shaft of warm light in what sometimes seems like a vast gloomy madhouse.

Not that we lack that warm light—I mean, the metaphorical warm light—here in London, which retains its indomitable Cockney cheerfulness and humour and therefore, I think, has resources denied to Hitler's anxious and depressed followers. I don't care how many countries these people conquer and loot, they'll never have much fun. If they managed to grab the whole earth—and don't worry, they won't—and could go swaggering and *heiling* and stamping wherever they pleased, they'd still be no better off, they'd still be anxious, gloomy and neurotic, because they're all wrong inside and their minds haven't been screwed down properly. You can't begin to turn hysterical ex-police spies into demi-gods, then all start spying on each other, and expect to have a roaring good time. It can't be done. You've sold yourself out. You've condemned yourself for life to a concentration camp. You're quietly going mad.

However, to get back to the air-raid life. So far last Saturday was our best example. I'm always wakened in the morning—though actually I'm nearly always awake by then—by the maid bringing in my mail and the newspapers and then drawing the curtains. Well, the timing on Saturday morning was perfect, for the alarm went just as she came in, so I took my letters and papers down to the basement, went through them down there, and by the time I had had breakfast and lit my first pipe, the All Clear went, and I returned upstairs. After which I settled down to a fruitful morning's work.

Good! Then a friend who lives near suggested we might have an hour's tennis at about five o'clock. Excellent! I needed some exercise. But then in the middle of the afternoon, the alarm went off again, and I thought, "Bang goes my tennis!" But no, there was some nice timing again, for the All Clear went just in time for me to change and slip round the corner for my tennis.

A typical incident in this afternoon's raid was that in the middle of it I became rather bored so came up from the basement and looked out of the dining-room window to see what was doing. Outside it was quiet and deserted, all the cheerful bustle of a fine Saturday afternoon having vanished. But then I heard the sound of some large approaching vehicle, and was curious to know what kind of fire engine or ambulance this majestic vehicle might be, so waited to see it pass my window. It was an enormous load—the biggest I've ever seen—of crates of bottled ale. And I felt as Wordsworth did when he beheld a rainbow in the sky—my heart leaped up. "Pass—thou noble beverage!" I cried. Not Goering and all his heroes, whose careful machine-gunning of children playing in fields and whose equally careful avoidance of our Hurricanes and Spitfires raise our appreciation of the heroic Teuton soul to a new level, not these mighty men and all their engines of destruction, I said to myself, can prevent the prompt dispatch to all parts of London of a good regular supply of bottled ale.

So I had my tennis, and then rested a bit, and had then to consider how to organise my evening. The point was, I was due in Whitehall at eleven-thirty to take part in a radio programme called "London After Dark." My job was to be the final commentator, looking out from a window in Whitehall across to the Cenotaph and the great government buildings, describing what I saw and ending with a noble peroration of some sort or other, and taking thundering good care, I was warned, to end at just the right fraction of a second that would enable the opening chimes of Big Ben, high above my head, to be heard across the Atlantic. Well, this sounded rather rough to me, even if there wasn't going to be any interference with our plans. However, if they wanted me to do it, then I must do it. But I had to be down there in Whitehall by eleven-thirty when the programme began, and if I stayed at home waiting for the appropriate time to set out and there happened to be an air raid just about then, I hadn't a dog's chance of getting down to Whitehall in time. I decided I'd better be somewhere in the neighbourhood, so I went to the theatre—to see a revue that was full of broad low comedy—and the place was packed to the roof, and the people there laughed so long and loud that even if there'd been an alarm I doubt if any of us would have heard it. (Last night, by the way, the alarm went during the performance, and as most of the audiences couldn't leave the theatres, they were given extra shows afterwards, and in one or two places, I'm told, members of the audiences then took a hand and gave turns themselves.) But to return to Saturday night. Once again, the timing was excellent, for I came out of the theatre, walked slowly along the dark crowded streets, and arrived at Whitehall just at the right time and also just as the alarm went. And there I was, for the next twenty-seven minutes, stuck in my large—I thought, much too large—open window in Whitehall, listening for the arrival of the bombers, waiting for the tiny red light at my elbow that would give me the cue to begin, wondering what the blazes I was going to say, now that I didn't even know how much time I would have or what was happening, except that I'd still have to time it so that Big Ben came in comfortably. All I can hope is that it didn't sound too much like the rather desperate enterprise it seemed to me.

When the broadcast was over and the B.B.C. expert who was looking after me was telephoning to know how we'd gone on, and we were lingering in that upstairs room, a whistling bomb, which sounded as if a steamboat was arriving vertically, came screaming down, landing in the city, and the caretaker, who was an old sailor and appeared to think that this was like the good old times, took us down to the air-raid shelter below, a shelter that was most efficiently constructed but rather too cold for comfort; and there we were joined by one or two other people, including a large smiling policeman who seemed to think, with the caretaker, that all this was rounding off the evening nicely; and we chatted of this and that for the next hour and a half, only interrupted by the sound of distant thuddings and the noises made by fire-engines in the neighbourhood. When the

All Clear went at last, my own situation was anything but all clear, because I was several long London miles from my own roof and bed, in which I was ready now to take a passionate interest; and several hundred thousand people in the centre of London appeared to be in the same predicament. After half an hour's wandering, I gave up the transport problem (which, by the way, has now been settled) and accepted an invitation to have a drink and sandwich, and did not see my own house until dawn was breaking.

In today's *News Chronicle*, Stanley Baron ends his daily diary with this paragraph:

Five hours in a suburban air-raid shelter, bombs falling before the warning and after the All Clears and silence in between, four violently rapid excursions from bed, a filthy morning temper. Then this from a demolition squad man, cheerfully sweeping out glass from a cavern of eddying dust: "Morning, guvner—'Itler's 'ousemaid, me!"

That's what the people are like here. In their prevailing good-temper, their adaptability, their humour and courage, their glorious, and their virtue shines like a great light in the darkness of this vast idiocy.

XXVIII. The Vexed Question of Britons in Hollywood

August 29, 1940

ONE TOPIC that has been finding its way into the press these days is the vexed question of the British actors, writers, film producers and directors, who are in the United States, chiefly in Hollywood, and show no signs of returning to this country. The discussion started when in the last issue of the *Sunday Dispatch*, Michael Balcon, one of our film producers who has stayed on here and done some good work, made a tremendous attack upon all these voluntary exiles, calling them "deserters." The point he makes is that Britain needs the services of these entertainment and propaganda experts just as much as she needs the services of all her skilled engineers, and that if a hundred of the finest aviation engineers deliberately walked out on us, to work, not necessarily for our benefit, in the United States, we should call them "deserters" and therefore he cannot call these self-exiled actors, writers, film producers anything but deserters. He is indeed very fierce with them, and his attack instantly produced an indignant defence, and various film stars of British birth have replied by telling the world how much they have been contributing to our Red Cross funds. It is, if you like, a storm in a tea-cup, but while the people taking part in this quarrel can command such publicity, we cannot afford to ignore it altogether, and so I propose to throw upon it the light of reason and commonsense.

Now in the first place, while I do not blame Mr. Balcon for being so angry and contemptuous, I do not myself share his anger and contempt—or at least not *all* of his contempt. And we must begin by doing what he was not careful to do, namely, we must make a distinction between those British writers, actors, film producers, etc. who had already, before this war broke out, decided to live and work in the United States, and those who did *not* arrive at this important decision until war was imminent or had actually started. With the first group, there can be no possible quarrel. They have discovered that they are happier or better-rewarded in the United States than they were in England, and so there is no more to be said. Britain has lost some charming and talented citizens; and I see no harm—and indeed, some good—in that transfer. Even with the second class, those who hurried out of this country presumably to avoid contact with this war, not necessarily because they are afraid of their skins but possibly because they are afraid of having little work to do, of losing the large salaries they have been enjoying, or because they felt the safety of the wives and children came first—I say, even with this rather unheroic group, I do not feel inclined to lose patience. I don't understand them, because I don't understand how sensitive men and women—and presumably they *are* sensitive, or they would not have been so successful as writers, actors, producers—can forget that natural piety, known to the humblest labouring folk, which compels you to return and stand by your own people in their time of trouble. I was myself far away in the United States during such crises as the Abyssinian campaign and Hitler's entry into Austria—which seem pretty small beer now but were devastating enough at the time—and though I was surrounded by delightful American friends, who were sympathetic to what we were feeling, I found it almost unbearable because I wanted to be back home. What I should feel like during *this*—if I were so far away—I can't imagine. I certainly don't envy these exiles, because either they are so insensitive that they feel nothing—and nobody wants to be such an unfeeling lout—or they *are* sensitive, which is more likely, and are feeling their isolation from their own folk, now making so glorious a stand, and are faced with a conflict inside their own minds that is as bad as, if not worse than, any possible Blitzkrieg they may be missing. Therefore it is absurd to be angry when what you really feel about these clever exiles is a mixture of wonder and pity. They don't know at first-hand how magnificent their own folk are. They don't realise that this country, even while facing such odds, is being born again, that there is stirring in these people a spirit that may ultimately change not only the face of Britain but the face of the whole world. To have missed that—just messing about in Hollywood—why, it's tragic, particularly as these artists can never feel part of our community again. They will remember the famous rebuke of the great Henry of France: "Go hang yourself, brave Crillon. We fought at Arques—and you were not there." To be deprived here of the services of so many brilliant stars of the films and stage may be a great nuisance to producers and a deprivation to a public that deserves every possible reward, but this loss is also our opportunity. We will create new stars. Here is a chance for unknown original talent of all kinds. We can find men and women—writers, actors, producers—whose art and character have been enlarged and enriched just because they have *not* been sun-bathing in Hollywood and Palm Springs but have been sharing the suffering, the courage, and the final glory of the common people of this land.

XXIX. There Is None of the Magnificent Chivalry of the Last War

September 1, 1940

OUR AIR-RAID life continues. We won't pretend it's a good life, because of course it isn't, but we're all making the best of it. Let me give you a homely example. In my house in London are a cook and two housemaids, young women all of them, with good experience and references, so that all three could easily obtain jobs elsewhere, away from the nightly raids. But not one of them has seriously grumbled and suggested she has had enough of it and is going to clear out. If they were having to put up with a twentieth part of this inconvenience—to say nothing of the danger—in peace time, the whole lot of them would probably have given notice long ago. But—though they say nothing about it—I know that they feel that this is their war job and they must do their best to see it through. On their free afternoons and evenings, they go across London to visit friends or go into the West End to a theatre or picture show, determined, as most of our people are—very sensibly, I think—not to lose hold of their ordinary life, to defy Goering and all his armies to keep them indoors.

I had another example, the other night, of our people's spirit. The London County Council, that gigantic municipal authority that has an annual revenue greater than that of many states, gave an invitation concert last Friday night in one of our very biggest halls, and as the London Philharmonic Orchestra were playing and I happen to have had some hand in saving this magnificent orchestra, I was asked to go and make a little speech. Well, no sooner had I mounted the conductor's rostrum and got under way than the sirens began wailing and screaming. "All right," I said, "there goes the air-raid alarm, ladies and gentlemen. But I propose to finish this speech."

At that there was a really tremendous outburst of cheering and applause and not a single person in that large hall, which was anything but an air-raid shelter, got up to go. I finished my speech—in which I told a story. It's from my own native country of Yorkshire. A Nazi parachutist landed in Yorkshire, found his way to a road, and there came across an old workman who was digging. The Nazi said, "Tell me, please, vich is the vay to Sheffield?" The old chap looked at him, then pointed down the road. "Yer go dahn there," he said, "until yer come to the cemetery, an' then yer turn to t'left, an' then yer keep on till yer come to t'gas works, an' then yer turn left again an' keep straight on. An' that'll bring yer back 'ere, lad, an' yer'll get t'same bloody answer."

That isn't a bad illustration of the spirit of the people. Anyhow, I finished my speech; we all had some drinks and sandwiches—for it was now the interval of the concert, and after that, though the air raid was still on, the orchestra carried on with the second half of the programme. And that's how London is taking it.

I notice that some of the New York papers have been saying that there are definite signs that in this war of nerves the Germans are losing badly. For once I must be allowed to cry, "What did I tell you?" Time after time I have pointed out that if the Nazis started a real war of nerves they would lose it, because their people can't stand up to these conditions as well as ours can. There are various reasons for this. One of them is that the German people have been living at too high a pressure for years now. They've been worked too hard, fed too badly, and alternately have been bullied or deceived by such thumping great lies as Goering's boast that no British bomber would ever find its way to Berlin and that even if one did it would be promptly destroyed. Our people haven't been told such fairy tales. On the contrary, they've been warned over and over again to expect the worst, so when a bad time comes they can stand up to it.

Then there's another thing, of the highest importance. In order to put it in its true perspective I'll tell an absolutely true little story. One day last week one of our boats went out to rescue some Nazi airmen from a bomber that had been brought down over the sea. Our people found three of these airmen sitting in their little rubber boat, very busy beating a fourth man, who was in the water, violently over the head and obviously trying to drown him. When our fellows asked the meaning of this most uncomradely behaviour, they explained that this fourth man was not really an airman but a member of the Gestapo, and that they were tired of him. It seems that now a Gestapo man is sent over with every section of German bombers, to see that the airmen are doing what they've been told to do and that there's no slackness and weakening. This may possibly explain why, in this new air warfare, there is none of that magnificent chivalry there was in the air combats of the last war, when all the airmen behaved to each other as if they were medieval knights. Now all that has vanished. For instance, the other day, one of our fighter pilots, who had had to bale out, was attacked while he was helplessly descending with his parachute by no less than three Messerschmitts, who riddled him with bullets. Such conduct would have been unthinkable in the last war, just as German airmen then would not have swooped down to machine-gun children playing in the fields. Probably under any circumstances most of these young Nazi airmen, who are inclined to be arrogant louts, could not be expected to behave as well as their fathers did, but we can now see there is another explanation of their completely unchivalrous, brutal, barbaric methods, and that is that even while fighting they are still under the eye of the dreaded Gestapo, which, filthily brutal itself, insists upon brutality from others. It is, no doubt, an efficient force—and the thought that it now swarms over at least half Europe, unchecked, is peculiarly horrible—and we can well believe that the Nazis owe a great deal to this army of cunning and unscrupulous brutes; but my own conviction is that in the long run the presence everywhere of this Gestapo will prove to be a liability and not an asset. Airmen— and sailors and soldiers—that find themselves continually spied upon, even when they are fighting, by the Gestapo, will sooner or later show themselves very decidedly inferior to airmen, sailors and soldiers who are trusted by their government to do their best. When a British bomber crew has to take to its rubber boat, you don't find three of them beating up the fourth. We don't have to spy upon our pilots and gunners, which is one reason at least why they are proving themselves as much better pilots and gunners than the Nazis. Even Germans, who will put up with more regimentation and bullying than any other people in the world, must be all heartily sick of this Gestapo, and I wouldn't be surprised if more and more members of this evil force are not discovered being clouted over the head in the immediate future. I venture, then, upon another prophecy, that the Nazi passion for spying upon everybody, including themselves—which has given the Gestapo such a stranglehold upon all the people under the Swastika— is now going to prove a liability instead of an asset.

Another Nazi trait, to be put alongside their passion for spying, is their sheer impudence. They are the most impudent gang that has ever achieved great political power in modern times. From the time when they coolly set fire to the Reichstag, claimed the communists had done it and so found an excuse for seizing power, they have shown the same astonishing impudence, the cheek of the devil. It is probably the result of having to deal at home with the most gullible people in Europe, so that they feel they can get away with anything. This is particularly obvious in their handling of what are called the rules of warfare. Now it is plainer than the nose on Hitler's face that from the start these so-called rules of warfare simply didn't exist for the Nazis. No plan they had ever made took the least notice of such rules. All their successes, from Norway down to France, were based on a complete ignoring of any possible international laws of civilised conflict. Thus, neutrality meant nothing to them. All their military successes have owed nearly everything to the flying start they have always had just because neutrality *did* mean nothing to them. The distinction between fortified and unfortified towns means nothing to them. The wholesale slaughter of helpless civilians means nothing to them. The time-old agreement that combatant troops must be dressed in uniform means nothing to them, for in the Low Countries they dropped thousands of parachute troops dressed as civilians and then—such is their superb impudence—actually had the audacity to complain that such troops, who were technically spies and could be treated as such, were being shot out of hand. Their idea is that they should be hampered by no rules whatever, but that we should be hampered by the maximum number of regulations, and fight with one hand tied behind our backs. Over and over they have repeatedly ignored the claims of the Red Cross Conventions, having deliberately torpedoed and fired upon ships plainly marked by the Red Cross, and having bombed and machine-gunned hospitals and ambulances.

All this is common knowledge. The Red Cross to the Nazis is merely an invitation to that form of easy attack which pleases them best. But now, such is their impudence, they have coolly proposed that they should employ in British waters no less than sixty-four Red Cross ships, presumably to rescue their airmen, and that such ships should be given complete immunity. This—from the very people who have recently been bombing and machine-gunning the boats of ours that have been actually engaged in the task of rescuing their own men! These so-called rescue ships of theirs could go more or less where they pleased, be used for observation, as we know their so-called Red Cross planes were —and probably for even more sinister activities, while we stood helplessly by. And this proposal came from the very people who have ignored every protest we have made against their flagrant disregard for the Red Cross, who went to the length of coming down deliberately to machine-gun nurses when such nurses tried to enter the boats from a hospital ship the Nazis sank. Sheer impudence can't go to greater lengths. This proposal—and the careful outcry that Goebbels will make now that it has been firmly rejected—are an insult to our intelligence, and indeed to the world's intelligence. It suggests that these Nazis, who can't decide whether soon they'll be owning the earth or hiding from the multitudes they have cruelly victimised, are rapidly losing what little mental balance they ever had.

XXX. First Anniversary of the War

September 3, 1940

Today we've been at war a whole year. Let us, then, look back. It's like looking back, from some high peak, on a whole wide range of mountains we've crossed. We see grim precipices and black gulfs, and also, here and there, shining summits that we have conquered and passed. Let us note some of the outstanding features of this vast wild landscape of war. And we must not only stare and wonder, but we must also *think*, for though we can easily spend too much time merely staring and wondering at this war, we can hardly spend too much time really *thinking* about it.

We'll begin with the worst event—the sudden, unexpected defeat and final capitulation of France. This is to my mind the most terrible event of the war so far, the one that haunts my imagination like some strange menacing dream. Over and over again I have to remind myself of the grim facts, to tell myself firmly that on the other side of the narrow straits of Dover a German army is in possession of the familiar friendly cliffs, that the Nazis are swaggering round Paris, that enormous French guns are being used to bombard our coasts. It is all nearly as incredible as it is horrible. It is this fall of France, this sudden disintegration under a few days' hammer strokes of a country that was thought to be an

[194]

impregnable fortress, that should be kept steadily in mind and carefully analysed by anyone who wishes to understand this war. France is this war's great object-lesson. Her lightning defeat represents the supreme triumph of the Nazi method—and that method is to apply the maximum possible force, used without scruple or mercy, to an antagonist who has already been weakened from within by every device of the Nazi propaganda and espionage system. Make no mistake about that. France was only defeated in the field after she had already been defeated in the bureaux and salons of Paris. Hitler could afford to throw in his last airplane, his last tank, because he knew that the brave men still opposing his armies had already been betrayed. His four columns —his planes, tanks, artillery, infantry—may have served him well, but he knew that even before he set them in action, his fifth column had already served him better still, and that France was doomed. We cannot afford to forget France, what happened to her and *why* it happened to her, for a single day.

Now let us turn from the black gulfs to some of the shining peaks. The most important military event for us was the triumphantly successful embarkation of the B.E.F. and other forces from Dunkirk. This last-minute snatch of a whole army, whose entire capture was undoubtedly part of the general plan, was immensely important not only because it robbed Hitler of a victory he had promised himself and the whole world, but also because it demonstrated, in the usual desperate dark hour, that Britain still possessed the power of rapid and brilliant improvisation, a national quality that serves us as German method and organisation serve them. After a procession of disheartening events, Dunkirk, with its audacity, its almost impudent unexpectedness, came like a flourish of trumpets. It was as if Drake and Nelson had returned to waken the islanders from their sleep.

Then, even more important, has been the success, right from the very hour of the invasion of the Low Countries to this present moment, of the Royal Air Force, which I am positive will be recognised, if it is not already recognised, as one of the greatest fighting forces in the history of the world, one of those groups of heroes who capture the imagination of man for ever. These young men, whether they go roaring over half Western Europe every night to find an exact target or come flashing out of the blue these mornings in their Spitfires and Hurricanes to deal out terror and destruction to the clumsy armadas of the Nazis, combine superb skill with audacity after a fashion that we thought had left this world. You have to go back to the Elizabethan sailors to find their equals. They are of the great race. They are living in some splendid saga that we on the ground can hardly begin to understand. I find it as difficult to praise these magnificent young men adequately as I do to think of their exploits at all without deep emotion. These youngsters, who go laughing and singing and charging about in their little cars with their girl friends, who are as modest as they are gallant, who are clean, clear-cut, chivalrous, are saving the civilised world, and the best form our gratitude can take is a determination that the world they save shall be worthy of such devotion, skill and heroism.

So much, then, for the fighting side of it all. Now let's turn to the political. Perhaps the most significant event in political Europe during this last year was Mr. Churchill's offer to complete union with France. Because this offer was made, no doubt after other appeals had been ignored, at the last minute of a dark hour, and more dramatic news immediately followed it, the significance of this offer has not, I think, been sufficiently widely appreciated. What is extremely important is the fact that this offer of complete federation should have been made at all. It marks the emergence of a new world in international politics.

I feel too that the presence here in Britain of the great governments of the conquered countries, along with their various legions of soldiers, airmen, sailors, is a fact whose significance has been under-estimated rather than over-estimated, and that this astonishing if still rather confused series of alliances must play its part in breaking down the old Europe. The Nazis are busy breaking down the old European system by imposing the same dread tyranny everywhere, but the free men who still defy them are equally busy, by the exercise not of tyranny but of mutual trust and co-operation, paving the way for a Europe that is no longer a cockpit of belligerent sovereign states.

[197]

Recent events on the other side of the Atlantic also seem to me to be pointing the way to a new world order of co-operating and not ruthlessly competing powers. As signposts, for example, there are the mutual defence talks between representatives of the United States and Canada. It is very hopeful that so much should have been done before the presidential election, which has immensely complicated the situation in the United States, and of which the Nazis hoped to take full advantage.

And now we come to the grandest peak of all, to the fact that has given me personally more hope for the future, not only of this war but of the world after the war, than any other fact—and that is the way in which the ordinary folk of this island have emerged as the real challengers of Nazism. When the real blitz-krieg began and the Nazi sprang like a tiger, then the British people, instead of losing heart, rose at once in spirit to meet the challenger. They came out of a sleep with which several of us had reproached them before this war began. They cried: "Give us some men to lead us," and at once they began to get the men, and these men told them to stop dreaming, to take their coats off and make a real fight of it, and roaring with enthusiasm the people waded in and began to show that democracy, when it's a real democracy and not a sham one, is just about as effete and decadent an antagonist as a wounded rhinoceros. They were told to go to it, and they went to it, with the result that during these summer months they achieved the greatest short-term war effort known to history, doing in a few months, as free men, what it took the Nazis, with their vast population of serfs, to do in years. The output of planes and munitions went soaring. The people responded triumphantly to every demand made upon them, and begged for more and greater demands. They worked till they reeled at the benches. Men and women who'd never worked hard with their hands in their lives demanded to be trained to do their share. Recruiting for every service went up by leaps and bounds. From all the great commonwealth of English-speaking peoples, from the ends of the earth, came young men for the fighting services, came instant offers of help. As the Nazi propaganda machine screamed its bestial threats, the spirit of these people rose and rose, and they demanded to defend this island to the last ditch. Then from feeling that they were living in a beleaguered fortress, they passed to the conviction that, right in the vast threatening face of the enemy, they were now living in the world's great base of freedom, from which would finally emerge the triumphant armies of liberty. With the coming of the ceaseless air attacks, which are still raging, these people found themselves in the very front line, and neither flinched nor whined, but cried again, "All right, come on. Let's see what you can do."

Unless it is understood that this is something more

than an heroic war effort, we underestimate its profound significance. What one must understand is that as soon as it was realised that this was indeed a people's war, immediately then vast new springs of courage, energy, power were suddenly tapped, to begin working miracles. And why? Because the people were awake at last, and such springs of courage, energy, power, exist in the people. In other words, here was democracy, not, as the dictators had hoped, tottering on its last legs, but coming roaring to life again, within sight once more of another great revolution of the human spirit. What the dictators sneered at and found it easy to defeat was not the real democracy but a shaky ruin of a sham old democracy that had long lost its old ardour, courage, and vision. But when these dictators hit hard enough and the ruin began falling, their hammer blows suddenly rang against steel, and that steel was the will of the people, who will not only defend what they have but will not rest again until they find their way to a nobler quality of life.

This then is my faith now, not only that Nazism will be finally defeated, as I believe it will be so that it will remain nothing but an evil memory and a lasting warning, but that already a new world order is being created out of the very stress and strain of this conflict, that men everywhere can take hope, for the new democracy is on the march. At last the British people are awake again, to astonish the world with their endurance, courage and good will—a great people, ready not only to meet any challenge but also to shape a new destiny for themselves and to help other peoples along the road to security, freedom and the good life.

And that is what one man has learned from this first year of war.

XXXI. What Are You to Make of People Like the Nazis?

September 5, 1940

I THINK NOW we're tending to take too little notice of Hitler's speeches, just as before the war and for the first two or three months of the war we tended to take his speeches too seriously. We made the mistake then of trying to discover in them some sensible reasoning and some clue to what the man was really wanting. But because they're crammed with nonsense of all kinds, that doesn't mean these speeches are of no value to us. Their appeal, of course, is entirely to the emotions of their audiences. Thus we can learn from them what Hitler wants Germany to *feel*, and can therefore deduce what he knows Germany *is* feeling and, indeed, something of what he himself is feeling.

Now notice the change of tone in his references to Britain. For a long time he and his gang jeered at us as a lot of effete decadent people, too lazy or cowardly to fight, who could be easily brushed aside by the young and virile Nazis and Fascists, whose Empire would collapse at a touch, whose day was done. That was the line. Stand aside, you weaklings! But now, please notice, this picture of the decadent pluto-democracy, tottering on its last shaky old legs, has vanished, and what has taken its place are references to us as bad, tough, piratical people who want to lord it over everybody else, from whose terrible unscrupulous tyranny Europe will have to be rescued by the nice kind Fuehrer, by the gentle Goering and his chivalrous air force, by the sweet-natured Himmler and his charming Gestapo and his delightful playmates, the Storm Troopers. The world, he tells us, must be set free from these arrogant British, whereas it is not long ago that the Nazi argument was that freedom was finished—it stank—and that the world must be carved up by the bright swords of the young virile peoples who no longer believed in freedom.

I'm not going to waste time pointing out the inconsistency of all this, for if there is anybody by now who does not realise that Nazi propaganda—and Hitler's speeches are part of the propaganda—has always ignored consistency, logic, reason, such a credulous person is not worth bothering about; but what is interesting here is the complete and unblushing reversal of attitude. If you don't stand up to this gang, they promptly kick you out of the way or beat you up and say it serves you right for being such a miserable weakling. But as soon as you do stand up to them, and return blow for blow, they drop all this tough talk and complain that they're really nice inoffensive people who don't mean any harm to anybody but just want to set everybody free, and this at the very time when they're busy over half Europe wringing the last drop of liberty out of the wretched conquered populations. In the same unblushing fashion, when France collapsed and they were happily gorging themselves on French food and drink, they announced a series of immediate dates for triumphant entries into London and victory parades for Berlin, and now, without turning a hair, they say that if Britain is prepared for a long war, they have been preparing for a still longer one, and not another word about triumphant entries and victory parades. In the same way, the vast German air force, they told us all, was to be used without mercy to bomb any defiant population into instant submission. They produced a film about Poland called the *Baptism of Fire*—I have seen it, and a most brutal, inhuman creation it is too—and actually used this film to terrify the neutrals they were proposing to invade; and afterwards carried out its threat by raining bombs upon Rotterdam and murdering tens of thousands of its civilian population. But now we are bad, tough people—night pirates—because we send over the R.A.F. every night into Germany. And this from the very people who've been screaming the most filthy threats at us for months and months.

What on earth are you to make of people of this kind, who are for ever alternately bullying and whining, who admit, when they think everybody is afraid of them, that they're ready to knock hell out of everybody without scruple or mercy, but then scream with rage or bewilderment the minute somebody begins to hit them back, who treat you with contempt if you try to live at peace with them, and then call you "war mongers" if you refuse at last to be humbugged, browbeaten and bullied any longer? What is this rotten spot in the German mind that makes reasonable co-operation with it impossible, that sets its owner always either bullying or whining? Whatever it is, it has done more mischief during the last seventy years than any other single factor in the modern European situation.

Meanwhile, we carry on. Here in London, the sirens, which are unpopular not because of their association with raids but simply as noises, go wailing at all odd hours, chiefly followed so far this week by the All Clear at surprisingly short intervals. During the day while the alarm is on, we may hear a high droning in the blue and sometimes hear distant gunfire, but we know that all round the edge of the vast London area the fighters and the ground defences are putting up something like a well of death for the raiding bombers. At night it is all more spectacular. The searchlights by the score make rapidly changing patterns in the sky. Sometimes there are many-coloured flares blazing like sudden comets. The horizon at times is almost volcanic with continuing flashes of anti-aircraft gunfire. And we are all rapidly discovering some rough-and-ready technique of carrying on with both our jobs and our pleasures under these novel conditions. It's surprising, on the whole, what little difference it makes.

XXXII. A General Stock-Taking

September 8, 1940

THIS is a good time to take general stock of the war situation. I don't pretend to be a military expert, but also I don't propose to apologise because I'm not a military expert. I had my suspicions about military experts before this war began, and nothing that's happened so far has made me shed any of those suspicions.

One of the very best known of our military critics proved to his own and everybody else's satisfaction that in modern warfare, between armies of anything like equal strength, the offensive was quite impossible, mere suicide. But that didn't prevent the Nazis trying the offensive, and wildly succeeding, in France. I admit that French resistance had been carefully undermined by fifth-column work, but that was something that most of our military experts had left out of account. Yet there was no excuse for their ignoring of the assault by propaganda, espionage and organised treachery, for Hitler had admitted that this was an essential part of his method. In Dr. Rauschning's book, *Hitler Speaks* [American title: *The Voice of Destruction*], Hitler is quoted as saying: "When I wage war . . . troops will suddenly appear, let us say, in Paris. They will wear French uniforms. The confusion will be beyond belief.

[206]

But I shall long have had relations with the men who will form a new Government—a Government to suit me. We shall find such men, we shall find them in every country. . . ." And again, Hitler is quoted as saying: "I shall never start a war without the certainty that a demoralised enemy will succumb to the first stroke of a single gigantic attack. When the enemy is demoralised from within, when he stands on the brink of revolution, when social unrest threatens—that is the right moment. A single blow must destroy him. Aerial attacks, stupendous in their mass effect, surprise, terror, sabotage, assassination from within, the murder of leading men, overwhelming attacks on all weak points of the enemy's defence, sudden attacks, all in the same second without regard for reserves or losses, that is the war of the future. . . ."* Well, there you have it, pretty plain speaking, though only intended, of course, for the ear of a confidant.

Incidentally, there is enough even in that single paragraph of talk to explain why it will be quite impossible to come to any kind of terms with this man and his gang, why no compromise peace can ever be considered, simply because to them there is no such possible condition of affairs as peace—they have never regarded themselves as being at peace since they first came to power, and if you try to compromise with them, all that will happen is that you will imagine that you are now at peace whereas they will quietly go on with their own

* By permission of G. P. Putnam's Sons, Publishers.

conception of war. There is absolutely no excuse now
for misunderstanding the Nazis—in my opinion, there
never was much excuse—for we have been given enough
glimpses of their appalling minds, cunning, treacherous,
and entirely without mercy. And it should be remembered—and I can only hope that every man in authority
on our side *is* remembering it day and night—that these
people have always succeeded by an amazing mixture of
brute force and sheer bluff, and that whatever a con-
ventional military mind considers impossible is just
what the Nazis are likely to attempt.

And now, with these things in mind, we come to a
consideration of this strangely delayed invasion. I say,
strangely delayed because although no doubt the German forces had to be reorganised to prepare for invasion, it is obvious that practically every advantage given
by the delay was ours and not theirs, enabling us to
bring our defences nearer to perfection. What is it that
has held up Hitler? I do not think myself it is simply
the sea. To think along that line is rather dangerous,
turning the sea into another Maginot Line. For myself,
I believe that what has made Hitler hesitant so far is
that now he is at last dealing with unknown factors.
I quoted him as saying: "When the enemy is demoralised from within," that is the right moment to strike.
But we British are anything but demoralised from
within. Our people's feeling of unity and confidence
was never stronger. Our morale, as Hitler must know,
is much higher now than that of the German people, in

spite of their spectacular victories. The more systematic, more accurate, and altogether deadlier raiding by the R.A.F. bombers is having more effect than the far more expensive raids of the Luftwaffe, which is losing trained men and good machines at an appalling rate. The preliminary war of nerves is going the wrong way for him, as I always said it would. When you come over, as a Nazi plane did last Friday, and swoop down and deliberately machine-gun civilians trying to take cover, killing a girl of nine, you don't encourage the British people to throw up the sponge but you make them angry and more determined than ever. Hitler has made a bad miscalculation. He should have lulled the British people to sleep instead of thoroughly wakening them up. Which makes me suspect once more that he doesn't understand the sort of people he's now dealing with, never having set eyes on them.

Again, not only has he failed completely to do any of this demoralising from within, which he himself recognises as one of the essential conditions of a successful offensive, but every important preliminary step in his long-term plan for invasion has been a failure. Thus, the British Expeditionary Force was to be captured at Dunkirk. It wasn't. The French Fleet was to be taken over and used against ours. It hasn't been. Instead, the Royal Navy is stronger than ever, and will be stronger still when the fifty destroyers from the United States are all on this side, doing convoy work, and releasing our big new destroyers for service—

and you may be sure, effective service—elsewhere. So next it was the turn of Goering's Air Force, now fortunately situated in being able to use advanced aerodromes along the French coast. This Air Force was given three tasks. It was to succeed, where the U-Boats had clearly failed, in blockading our shores, by attacking convoys, docks, etc. Then by attacking industrial centres, it was to paralyse our great war effort, bringing down with a run our output of planes and munitions. Thirdly, it had, at no matter what immediate cost to itself in planes and men, to acquire a complete ascendancy over the R.A.F. and especially to drive the dreaded fighters, whose range is limited, from all their aerodromes anywhere near the coast, or alternatively to denude the greater part of the country of fighters by attracting all available squadrons to the south-east corner, against which nearly all the heavy attacks have been directed.

It would, of course, be absurd to pretend that these raids at all hours, delivered by great masses of machines, have had no effect at all. Naturally, there has been damage to property, some loss of life, and here and there some fall in output. But it can be said without hesitation that in not one of its main tasks has the German Air Force succeeded at all, and that its losses in highly trained men and expensive machines have been enormous. The game has simply not been worth the candle. It is possible, it is indeed very likely, that still heavier attacks, gigantic mass raids, have been planned, and it will be anything but pleasant for us when they arrive, but the prospect is even more unpleasant for the raiders, faced as they will be by a completely unbroken R.A.F. and by ground defences that are becoming more and more accurate every day.

Meanwhile, however, our own raids deep into Germany are reported to be giving the Nazis a very bad headache. There are several reasons for this. Firstly, the choice of targets—and this bombing of ours is nothing if not systematic—is part of a very carefully planned and brilliant campaign for the destruction of Germany's war industries, and both the men and the machines are better than those used in the German raids here. Secondly, the German people had been assured over and over again that although their machines could bomb anybody and everything, they were not to be bombed back—a nice convenient arrangement; and now they know only too well that these assurances and boasts were worth nothing. Thirdly, the Nazis cannot understand how so much rapid and accurate information about the damage done in these raids reaches London, and they realise that they have no monopoly of espionage and secret service. Indeed, their position in this respect will clearly go from bad to worse, for you cannot bully and beat up other people for years without making a great many determined enemies, and now it looks as if the Nazis are about to reap the harvest of their evil sowing of treachery, violence and terror.

This will apply even more outside German territory proper, in all the countries recently conquered by the

Nazis. We have heard a great deal about this terrifically long coastline, from Narvik down to Biarritz, that the Nazis hold, and from which they threaten us, in a great arc of coast over three thousand miles long. But this cuts both ways. These three thousand miles have to be held and defended, and in the face not only of an efficient and menacing British Navy, Air Force and Army, but also of a largely sullen, hostile and rebellious local population. Hitler has admittedly a very large army indeed, possibly by now even ten or eleven millions of more or less trained men. But he has also a great deal to do with that army. He has to man and defend, to a depth of twenty or thirty miles, a coastline of three thousand miles, which can be raided anywhere by an enemy who commands the sea. On land he has to keep an eye on the Czechs and the Poles, which can't be done without armed forces. Further east he has to keep a large armed force on the Russian and Balkan frontiers. Even at home the Storm Troopers and Gestapo must swallow a very large number of fit trained men. Then if on top of all this, he proposes to try an invasion of Britain, now bristling with men and guns, and at the same time prepares for adventures in North Africa, alongside an ally, Italy, that has less and less stomach for a really tough campaign and might easily collapse under sudden pressure, for all his millions and millions of marching robots, Herr Hitler has all his work cut out.

We don't pretend to be out of the wood yet. We're

in it still, with all manner of menacing shadows round us, but if we are, then—by thunder—so are the Nazis for all their lightning conquests. The autumn draws nearer, and behind it looms the dark gaunt face of Winter; the British blockade is not only unbroken but tightens its grip; the Royal Air Force, with more men and machines every day, roams farther and farther afield and cannot be stopped; the islanders set their jaws and defy his bombers, which fall through the air like rotten fruit; and the terrible game of total war, which these evil men planned and once rejoiced in, will be played to a finish.

XXXIII. The Colossal Panorama
of a Defiant City

September 10, 1940

IN ONE of our newspapers this morning, there is a cable dispatch from their New York Correspondent, which begins: "Front pages of newspapers here are black with headlines describing death and destruction in London and lurid with boasts and threats coming from Germany."

They are doing it, of course, because they feel it's good journalism—"London Now a Hell on Earth": that's one of the great stories of the century. Well, it may be good journalism—but nevertheless it's just playing the Nazi game. It's all part of the war of nerves. They've been screaming at us for some time now, without much result. And don't make any mistake. It's the people who are screaming what they're going to do, the people who have to magnify the stupid destruction of workmen's houses and tenements into a great military victory, whose nerves are failing them. We've only got to stick it—and sooner or later this gang of neurotic butchers will be on the run.

So much for that.

Well, what's it like in this so-called "hell on earth"? To begin with, it's a long way from being a hell on earth yet, except of course in certain widely separated

[214]

places at certain moments. I'm here, and I ought to know. Also, I know what hells on earth are—I've seen them. The Somme, Verdun, Vimy Ridge, Passchendaele —those were real hells on earth, where tens of thousands of magnificent young men were withered away in a morning. We haven't got anywhere near that yet. These recent big raids, indiscriminate, vindictive and fundamentally stupid, like the plungings and lashings about of an enormous tormented beast robbed of its prey, have caught the world's imagination, and the fact that they have done this is itself a tribute to the might and majesty of London itself—

> the resort and mart of all the earth,
> Chequered with all complexions of mankind—

or as a poet cried in the middle ages, when nobody had heard of Berlin: "London, thou flower of cities all."

I am not myself a Londoner, though I have lived here on and off for twenty years, but during these last few days I've been proud to feel myself a Londoner. I should think even these young Nazi airmen, who are notoriously not very sensitive types, must have been troubled by a feeling of awe as they caught glimpses far below them of the ancient mighty capital city whose contributions, by way of government and law, arts and sciences, to the world civilisation have been incalculably vast. Time after time, during these last few days, I have gone up to high places, my own roof and other roofs, at dusk, during the night, and at dawn, to stare at the

colossal panorama of the defiant city. This morning, for
example, at daybreak, I climbed to my own roof, which
is very high up on top of London's steepest hill, and
stared about me in the chill sweet dawn, feeling most
deeply moved. There, lead-coloured in that sunless early
glimmer, was every familiar monument, not one land-
mark of the city missing, all there—as if standing to at
reveille as we used to do in the trenches at this hour; but
far away, dramatic in their sharp vermilion and orange,
were curling tongues of fire. I had gone up before,
fairly early in the night, but then had only seen a distant faint glow or two of fire, like minor wounds on
that colossal body of the city, which was raying out its
searchlights and keeping the horizon pulsating with
flashes of gunfire.

On Sunday night it was much more spectacular, when
I went up very high in central London and watched
the fires that for hours had cast a rosy glow over half
the sky and turned the upper storeys of those whitish
London terraces a bright pink. From where I watched,
the greatest of the fires was just behind St. Paul's, which
was carefully silhouetted in dead black against the red
glare of the flames and the orange-pink of the smoke.
It stood there like a symbol, with its unbroken dome
and towering cross, of an enduring civilisation of reason
and Christian ethics against a red menacing glare of un-
reason, destruction and savagery. You get the same
significant contrast when you listen to and compare the
voices and speeches of Winston Churchill and Adolf

Hitler, one a gallant reasonable man, seriously weighing evidence and considering chances, and the other a screaming raving neurotic, hardly knowing what he's saying but mad with violence and hate. In the other half of the sky, where the blue night still held sway, the searchlights made rapidly changing patterns, now coming together sharply and now swinging in wide arcs, trying to locate the tiny objects that were droning round and round before dropping, quite indiscriminately, their cargoes of destruction and death. It was much later, it was daylight, in fact, when I started on my way home mingling with the crowds, some of whom, like me, were going home after their night's work, and others emerging to begin their day's work. Transport is still difficult after these long raids, and this is probably our chief ground problem now, but I've no doubt whatever that soon, ways and means will be found to speed it up. After various bouts of walking and waiting, I managed to get a bus or two to help me on my way. The people were all wonderfully patient and good. They were tired, of course, but in no way fearful or cast-down or even fretful. We passed near—and had to slow up—by a scene of most fantastic destruction, where an exceptionally heavy bomb must have fallen during the night, for not only were several houses completely wrecked but, immediately next door to this wreckage, a large London bus had been half flattened out and hurled against the side of a building, clean up in the air, for now one end of it was resting against the second storey,

[217]

just as if it had been a little piece of tin that you picked up and hurled against a wall with such force that it stuck there. Fortunately, this bus had been completely empty at the time. Well, we all had a good look, in my bus, at this spectacle, but in spite of the long hours of danger and waiting and weariness, nobody was at all overcome—there were merely murmurs of indignation.

The elaborate A.R.P. services, which were rather sneered at for some time, have proved themselves invaluable and heroic during these nights, not only because they are extremely well organised but also because the quality of service given by the men and women acting as air wardens, fire fighters, and as members of emergency squads, has been really magnificent, something that could not be bought with money, that springs out of a deep devotion to and love of this great city and its people. If the intention of the Nazis in the use of this indiscriminate bombing, in which bombs of the heaviest calibre have been dropped anywhere and everywhere, is simply to terrorise the people of London, then they are wasting men, machines and high explosives. So long as our people feel they can hit back—and we're going to hit back harder and harder—Goering will never bomb them into suing for terms even if he sends over, night after night, every machine he's got.

In the meantime, of course, he sets some of us some pretty little problems. I have no outside air-raid shelter, so we go down into the basement, and I've had one of the rooms down there reinforced and shored up with heavy timbers. It won't stand a direct hit, of course—a direct hit with a bomb of any size, and it's good-bye—but we're hoping that if a bomb comes near and brings down the upper parts of the house, this reinforced basement will be strong enough to withstand the sudden weight of debris. I was buried alive and had to be dug out in the last war, and it'll be odd if it happens to me all over again in this war—and at home, in my own house too!

What a lot of lunacy it is, isn't it? Add one part sheer wickedness to about a hundred parts downright stupidity and mental laziness, and suddenly you find yourself spending your time in the basement wondering if some young idiot, twelve thousand feet above you, is going to press a button and perhaps blot you out, and all for the sake of the greater glory of an ex-paper-hanging Austrian police spy who probably isn't right in his head.

But I was talking of the problems we have to solve now. For example. I have to be in London, blitzkrieg or no blitzkrieg, to do my work—such as broadcasting, though that's not all I do, by a long chalk. And because I'm in London, my wife, who is otherwise a very sensible woman, thinks that *she* ought to be in London, as the children are now all going back to school, still in England, but well away from all these doings. Now if both of us are in London, still installed in our house, the cook and housemaid think that *they* ought to stay in London. And my secretary, who has a cottage in the country to which she could go, thinks that *she* ought to stay on in London. And so it goes on. With the result that I find myself surrounded by women, who actually are all much calmer than I am, but that doesn't prevent my feeling that I'm responsible for their being here, and if anything did happen to one of them, I know I'd feel guilty about it.

Then again, it's all so complicated. Last night, they all rushed to put on trousers—these air raids are simply being used as an excuse by Englishwomen to put on trousers—and down they came, bringing mattresses and pillows, to the shelter room in the basement, with the result that they filled it—and anyhow I felt I was intruding in this very feminine atmosphere—so I put a mattress in a kind of little cubby-hole corner under the stairs and got down there; and though it was rather stuffy and smelt of mice and camphor and I could hear a lot of sinister bumps and bangs and the house gave an occasional little shiver—as well it might, poor old house—I somehow managed to obtain several hours' sleep. At the same old time in the morning, the letters were there, the newspapers were there, my breakfast was there, and we were all there, carrying on.

They are saying in London today that this is the critical fortnight, and that the Nazis, stung by the obvious failure of their previous threats and boasts, are about to make a major move, attempting invasion. That's one interpretation, though I would have thought that another was that this aerial blitzkrieg has been put in as a kind of noisy cover while one set of plans is scrapped

[220]

to make way for another set of plans. I don't know. What I do know is that the latest high Nazi view— which is that this blitz will result in the resignation of the present government here, is just about the silliest put forward yet; and that the expression of such wildly nonsensical notions, coupled with this wildly indiscriminate bombing, suggests that the Nazi leaders are much worried men.

XXXIV. You Eat and Drink as Usual, for These Are Hungry Times

September 12, 1940

NOT MANY people in London had much sleep last night—though I must say I didn't do too badly myself, for I must have had two or three hours' sleep, of a broken kind, down in the basement, and then an hour or so in bed after the All Clear was sounded—but nobody was grumbling this morning, because last night what kept people awake was not the bombs but the anti-aircraft barrage, keeping the bombers away. This was the loudest barrage I've heard since the battles in France of the last war. It began almost as soon as the sirens went, raged for hours and hours, and was simply terrific. We all had the impression, down in our basement, that much bigger guns had come into action, for there were deeper notes than before. Some bombs were dropped, of course, but I don't remember hearing one, so loud, fierce and continuous was the barrage. It seemed impossible that anything could live in the areas of sky they were blasting, and that must have been the conclusion of many of the Nazi pilots, who were turned back.

This morning the streets and some of the gardens in our part of the city were littered with pieces of shell casing. Our cook found one in our own back garden and is proud of her souvenir. It says much for the spirit of the London people that in spite of the fact that this immense shelling robbed them of their sleep and must have brought down tons of bits of metal on the city, making movement in the streets quite dangerous, everybody has been jubilant today, saying: "Did you hear it last night? That's the stuff to give 'em."

If Hitler is really seriously considering invasion during the next few days, he's showing no trace of his usual insight into the moods of his opponents, for the people here are now full of fighting spirit and ready to hit back with everything they've got. And yet we read that so successful has been the Nazi propaganda among their own troops now waiting to attack Britain that the rank and file believe they are in for an easy walkover. Which would be laughable if the lives of hundreds of thousands of human beings weren't involved. From our Prime Minister we get the sort of grim fighting speech he gave us last night. I couldn't help feeling, though, that some of his speech was as much intended for Hitler's ears as it was for ours, telling him very plainly that we knew exactly what he was up to and were making our plans accordingly.

There is one new factor that makes me feel very hopeful in this present tremendous crisis. Not the fine spirit of the ordinary people here. I've never had the slightest doubt of that—I know our people. No, the new factor that makes me feel so hopeful is that our natural inventiveness and resourcefulness are beginning to make themselves felt. Because our governing classes are so inclined to cling to traditions, and the ordinary people themselves are so apparently slow-moving, the world is apt to forget that in actual fact we are an unusually inventive people, as our record in science, industry, and war easily proves. In this war we started a long way behind the Germans, who'd been thinking about nothing but making war for years and had been piling up material. But the Germans, though remarkable adapters and organisers, are not an unusually inventive and resourceful people, and that is why I have always felt that once we swung properly into action, using all our best brains, we should easily outstrip them. And there seems to me now distinct signs that this is precisely what we're beginning to do. From the first, of course, both our bombers and fighters have been better than theirs; and then again our carefully systematic bombing of the German war industries and transport has been far better planned and executed than their bombing campaign here. But there is much newer evidence than that. Thus, the R.A.F.'s substitution of millions of small self-igniting cards for the usual incendiary bombs, directed against military objectives in the German forests, has been followed by very good results. Again, last night's sudden and entire change of ground defence against bombers, in which, I understand, more and heavier guns played their part, shows that this inventiveness and resourcefulness, and the power of rapid improvisation for which we have always been famous, are all rapidly coming into play. I shall be extremely surprised, particularly if Hitler decides to risk an attempt at invasion, if further examples of invention and resource don't come tumbling out of the bag.

Meanwhile, with Mr. Churchill's grave warning ringing in our ears, we remain on the alert and continue to lead our air-raid life. For a comparative few—far fewer, of course, than were ever anticipated at the beginning of the war, when enormous casualty lists were expected—this has been a tragic week, and most of us know somebody who has met, one of these nights, horrible tragedy, destruction and death, face to face. But for the rest of us, numbering some millions, it has been a week of odd moments of strain, when bombs were unpleasantly near, with considerable periods of tiredness and inconvenience. I suppose I notice the tiredness as much as most because it happens that I'm working at full pressure and can't slacken down. The inconvenience, of course, is obvious to everybody. Yet the marvel to me is how little downright interruption to our life there is. You contrive to do, somehow, all the more important things you've undertaken to do. My wife, for example, has been busy buying the children's winter clothes this week. The newspapers arrive in the morning and in the evening. The radio programmes are in full swing, even if theatrical and film shows are cut down. You eat and drink as usual, perhaps rather more than usual, for these are hungry times. You keep most of your appointments, either for business or pleasure. In fact, you carry on, happily conscious of the fact that you are in the midst of a great battle and appear to be winning it. And I'll bet that's more than Goering can say.

XXXV. Prepared for Anything—with a Word About Propaganda

September 15, 1940

L AST FRIDAY, the 13th, was my birthday, and it had been arranged that I should go down to my sister-in-law's pleasant little country house, where an excellent steak-and-kidney pudding was waiting for me. Although this house is only eighty or ninety miles from London, it seemed to take me most of Friday to get there, not because the railway service was dislocated—so far as I could see, it wasn't, and we travelled by the usual route so obviously there had been no bombs along that line— but because the early morning air-raid alarm made me miss the fast train and I was landed with a slow brute, stopping at every possible station and halt. A great many children were also being evacuated from London that day, and we kept travelling alongside a whole trainload of them, twittering away like Cockney sparrows. There were a lot of evacuated children in the village where I stayed. And what were they playing at? They were playing at air raids.

There in that charming old village I had what they called "thirty-six hours' peace and quietness," and if peace and quietness means the absence of sirens, bombs and barrages, they were right. But strictly speaking, it was anything but quiet during the day, for there is an

R.A.F. training establishment in the neighbourhood, with the result that all day the sky shuddered with the tearing, rending sound of the training planes, which are far noisier than the service machines. Some of these lads seemed to be going up and ripping the sky in two as if it were blue calico. But I managed to have two whole nights in bed, fast asleep too, so feel ready to face another week of little sleep and long working hours.

What this week will bring forth, no man knows. In spite of our bombers' colossal smashing strokes on all the ports facing us, the attempt may be made to invade us, before the autumn gales begin and there are mountainous tides in the Channel. When I remember the unpleasant hours I've spent crossing from the Hook of Holland to Harwich, from Ostend to Dover, Calais and Boulogne to Folkestone, Dieppe to Newhaven, with the ships I've been in vainly trying to make the harbour mouths—and nobody trying to stop us, with everybody on our side—I can't help wondering what kind of hellish voyage it's going to be in transports and barges that have not only wind and weather but the full force of the Navy, Air Force, and Army against them. And then behind these formidable forces, all waiting on the coast to receive you—and how those boys back from Dunkirk are just waiting!—you have not crowds of welcoming cheering fifth columnists but an absolutely hostile angry population, and in a higgledy-piggledy island where there are no long straight roads but deep twisting lanes where you can be ambushed every few hundred yards. And your retreat has been cut off, and the Fatherland has vanished beyond the cruel grey seas. I must say that if I were a German soldier I should take a very forlorn view of this enterprise and beg to be allowed to do my invading elsewhere, even if it were across the waterless deserts of North Africa.

But there it is—the attempt may be made at any time, by this power-crazy gang who piled up their dead in sickening heaps in Flanders, like robots flung into a furnace, and have not since had even the decency towards their own people to admit their losses, telling their wretched dupes that they lost a mere handful when in fact hundreds and hundreds of thousands of German lads perished within a few days. There must be some limit to the self-deception of the Germans. We know how, in order to hide the truth about their losses, the German Air Force makes its raids here by machines and men selected from many different squadrons, but even so, when a hundred machines and their crews are lost in a day and the men are told they only lost ten, even the Germans must begin to smell a rat. In the long run that game, like all these Nazi games, can't pay. You can't fool all the people all the time. Our careful conservatism in our estimates, our deliberate understatements, may be poor propaganda, but surely unless the whole world is rapidly becoming half-witted, this is the better policy. And when we do claim superiority, we are always willing to give sensible reasons for that claim.

[229]

For example, is it true that the R.A.F. is doing far more vital damage in Nazi territory night after night than the German bombers are doing here? The answer is, Yes it is true, in spite of the fact that the German bombers have such a small distance to travel to reach us, and that probably more of them are being used. Then why, in spite of these serious disadvantages, should we have the superiority? Here are the reasons. The R.A.F. are far better navigators and have had far more practise. Their heavy night bombers are much better machines than the German equivalent, having been constructed with more care, at a far greater cost, and of much better material. Again, our bomb sights are much better than the ones used by the Nazis. Again—to quote an expert—"our bombs are more expensive, more carefully made, and much more destructive than the German bombs." There you have it. So far the fight between the Luftwaffe and the Royal Air Force has been a battle between quantity, in which the Nazis excel, and quality, in which we excel. If we can keep the same *quality* of men and machines and arrive at the same *quantity* as the Nazis, the Nazi game is up—they'll be blown clean out of the sky—and they know it, hence all these recent desperate moves, screams and threats, terror bombing, mad-dog tactics. That is why now we have to be prepared for *anything* here, for there is nothing these lunatics won't try now they know that time is against them and that it is a quick victory or nothing.

The prospect is anything but a pleasant one, but it is

infinitely preferable to the prospect of a Nazi-ridden world, with everybody kow-towing to these swaggering, lying brutes; and people here are quite prepared to endure anything rather than come to terms with this gang. The fabric of London is shaken and scarred whereas that of Paris is hardly touched, but who would be a citizen of Paris now rather than a citizen of London? One city, though untouched, is now dead, a mausoleum of the hopes of men, whereas the other, our London, is gloriously alive, and even if its body should be reduced to ruin and ashes, its soul will endure for ever in the hearts and imaginations of men. But London doesn't look like ruin and ashes yet, not by a thundering long chalk, and I'll wager it'll outlast all Hitler's schemes.

And now, a word about propaganda. I receive a good many letters, especially from my radio listeners in the United States, saying something like this: "I enjoy your talks very much, though of course I realise that they are only propaganda." Now, I'd like to get this straightened out. In one sense my talks *are* propaganda, but in another sense they are definitely *not* propaganda. I'll explain exactly what I mean. I'm an Englishman and what is more I have always been a determined anti-Nazi, long opposed to any talk of appeasement or trying to come to any compromise with these people. I have always believed, right from the moment they came to power, that their main object was conquest, without war if possible but with war if necessary. I called them as many hard names before this war as I've done since. In addition, I disagreed most bitterly with the pre-war British policy and said so in public, over and over again. That is my position—and if it makes me a propagandist, then my talks are propaganda; though I'll add that I can't believe that anybody can really be neutral about such people. Real detachment is impossible. Either you're for them or against them, as they themselves know very well. Well, I'm against them and always have been. But in the real sense of the word as it's used now, this does not make me a propagandist and I don't talk propaganda in the sense that the radio commentators in Germany talk propaganda. The difference is this: their talks are all part of a general campaign of propaganda, a campaign that they know is just as important as the work of their air forces and armies. It is a campaign that is just as carefully planned as any other, and has its own strategy and tactics. Each talk that goes out is itself a tiny raid or advance, an essential if small part of the general campaign. But my talks are *not* part of any such campaign, which with us, rightly or wrongly, does not exist. So long as I do not give information that might be useful to the enemy, I am free to say what I please. I am simply a private person giving his impression of what is happening. I have no official standing, privileges or salary. The B.B.C. pays me just as it would if I were a pianist or a singer taking part in its programme. But that is all. No official tells me what to say. There are no strategy and tactics in the background, no propaganda campaign at all. I am just as free to express my own opinion as any American commentator here in London. Indeed, in one sense I think I am freer than some of my colleagues from the United States—though here I must make an exception of the radio commentators of the big American networks here, who are doing a grand fair job—whether they are newspaper or radio men, and this is why. Nobody suggests to me that I have to make it exciting all the time. Nobody says: "Come on, Priestley, let's have a bit more punch in it, a bit more drama, more colour, more excitement."

After all, while we're on the subject of propaganda, isn't there a third kind that nobody mentions, not pro-Nazi, not pro-British, but pro-excitement, pro-sensation? Isn't it possible, rather innocently, to falsify the picture not because you've got a bias for one side or the other but because you can't help jazzing and hotting it up all the time, because you've been sent a long way to do a job—and, to be fair, may be doing that job at considerable personal risk—and feel that unless everything you write or say over the air is sizzling hot with excitement and breathless sensationalism, you're not really doing your job? And doesn't this attitude, although there may be the friendliest feelings towards Britain behind it, tend to help the Nazis to play *their* game?

Life here is grim, but no worse than that. If the decent little folk who've been bombed night after night, who've lost friends and relatives, who've seen the ruins of what were once their homes, can take it easy and don't go round screaming about "great doomed cities" and "hells on earth," there's no need for anybody else—except the Goebbels gang—to do any screaming. Steady and easy does it. And we'll yet hammer some cold sense into these neurotic brutes.

XXXVI. These Are Puzzling and
Puzzled Men

September 17, 1940

LAST NIGHT I had a very lucky escape. Yesterday morning I moved into an hotel, taking enough of my personal belongings—clothes, writing materials, pipes, and tobacco—to last me at least several weeks. And I spent the afternoon in this hotel, during various air-raid warnings, working on a film with a colleague. Then in the early evening I received a message from the B.B.C. asking me if I'd mind giving a special talk on the overseas programme on the spirit of London during the raids. I said I would but wasn't too pleased about it because Monday is one of my free nights and I was hoping to get to bed early. However, I prepared the talk and left my hotel in good time to be ready on the spot.

The night's air raid began and the bombs sounded loud and near. They seemed to be concentrating on our part of London. The rumours of what was happening outside began to circulate, as usual, and soon I heard that an hotel had been hit. A little later I heard that *my* hotel had been hit, not all of it, apparently, but one wing. I spent some odd moments then wondering *which* wing had been hit. After a not very comfortable night, during which I interrupted some mere dozing by get-

ting up in the weird small hours, when I watched the
return of some heroic fire-fighters, some of whose comrades had been killed and wounded only an hour before,
there were, of course, more rumours about what had
been hit during the night. Popping up as I did between
two periods of broken sleep, this was a strange, dream-
like scene—exchanging fantastic news with strangers, in
the deepest hour of the night, in the heart of the defiant city, familiar streets and squares taking their place
in this foul, mad battle. Then when it was full daylight
I went out into the shattered streets, to discover what
had happened to my hotel. Most of it was there. But
not, I soon discovered, the wing, where my room was.
Had I not been asked to do that special talk and had
gone to bed early—well . . . It would have been, to
say the least of it, something of a shock, and it is more
than likely I would have found myself sharing my bed-
room with a ton or two of débris. As it is, here I am,
and now my only worry is whether I am going to see
any of those handsome suits, shirts, socks again, and
especially those beautifully broken-in and friendly pipes.

I feel this is almost a moral tale, a lesson for the
young and lazy, for if I had refused to do a bit of extra
work and had chosen to sleep instead—*bang* would have
come that bomb down on me! But if the people here
imagine that they can now ask me to do extra talks at
all hours of day and night, they're wrong.

I wouldn't have missed the sight of that hotel entrance this morning for anything. Everybody had been

[236]

evacuated out of it during the night, of course, until the damage had been carefully surveyed. Now, when I arrived, the staff were back and the guests were returning, from various nearby shelters, and there was a general air of the successful conclusion—say, the landing on a well-watered tropical island of a recent shipwreck. The guests, I must admit, were hardly looking their best, but there—standing in the dead centre of the entrance hall—was the little assistant manager, as immaculately dressed as ever in his morning coat, striped trousers, irreproachable linen. His manner was as completely unruffled as his appearance. His tone was still as smooth as cream. "Good morning, madam. Good morning, sir. I trust you were able to sleep. Let me see, your room is—so-and-so. Yes, I'm afraid you won't be able to return there. No, sir, no breakfast, I'm afraid, but we hope to be able to arrange lunch. Yes, sir, the barber's shop is open and will be very glad to attend to you. *Good* morning, madam. Yes, *very* troublesome night. Perhaps you'd like to rest in the lounge."

I hope you discover in all this, as I certainly do, a kind of heroism, just as much to be admired in its smooth, morning-coat-and-striped-trousers style, as the cheerful dauntless heroism of so many of our East End folk, and though far below it in the scale of cold courage and sense of duty, belonging to the same order as the astonishing heroism of those squads of soldiers who deal with the time bombs, whose leader, Lieutenant Davies, who drove that unexploded ton bomb from St. Paul's to Hackney Marches, seems to me to deserve several Victoria Crosses.

I was equally impressed by the appearance and manner of all the folk I saw this morning picking their way along the littered and partly shattered streets around this hotel. They *ought*—according to the combined calculations of Hitler, Goering, and Goebbels—to have been emerging pale, shaken, shivering with fright, the last tottering victims of the century's great bully, but the fact remains that they were doing nothing of the kind. They hadn't had a very comfortable night and might be in for an irritating, closed-up kind of day, but they showed no trace of alarm, looked about them with curiosity, and went about their day's business as best they could, far less at odds with life than the miserable haunted men who have spilt their wickedness over the world, the German outlaws, for that is what they really are; who not only seek power at all costs, but who can never be brought within any possible civilised system, who will always put themselves outside any reasonable world order, because they always have been and never can be anything else but outlaws.

At the moment they seem to be both puzzled and puzzling outlaws. They are puzzling because it is extremely hard to fit their recent activities into any suggestion of a rational pattern. Either they are working to perfect some scheme so subtle and far-reaching that it is beyond our wits, or they are behaving with great stupidity. For example, this bombing of London. In the

[238]

first place, why do it at all? What has been gained by it, from their point of view? Some disorganisation of our life here, of course, and homelessness, injury, and death for some thousands of innocent citizens. Presumably this is intended to do two things: first, to paralyse our war effort, secondly, to break the morale of the London citizen, so that he will demand that his government will sue for peace. But attacks on London cannot paralyse our war effort. Last night a number of bombs were dropped in the West End area where I am sitting at this moment, but not one 'plane, one gun, one shell is being held up in its manufacture because high explosives are being dropped on blocks of flats, hairdressing establishments, hotels, or outfitters' shops. This must be as obvious to the Nazis as it is to us.

Therefore, it must be reason Number Two—the effect upon morale—that must be the real reason for these attacks. So let us have a look at that. It is now common knowledge—outside Germany and Italy, where they are seriously told that we are all in a state of panic—that the morale of the London citizens, even those in the East End who have suffered the most, has been heightened rather than depressed by these foul, indiscriminate attacks. But why should they have expected anything else? I don't say this because I know our people are courageous and tenacious. They are, but that is rather beside the point. I don't believe that *any* people who have been rendered homeless, who have seen their relatives and friends killed and wounded, would say, "Let's give in. We've had enough of this." On the contrary, so long as they had any power at all of hitting back—and we have a daily increasing power of hitting back—they would want to hit back harder than ever, and would grow angrier and more determined. That is human nature, and we don't expect anything else. We ourselves don't believe in these terror tactics, and all our bombing is conducted on quite different principles. It is possible that if the Nazis had confined their bombing to the poorer quarters of London and had obviously left the richer parts alone, they might have created an awkward situation and something like disunity might have been produced. But instead of that—and I for one fully expected them to do that—they take pains to spread their attacks all over the capital, dropping nearly as many bombs on the West End as they have done on the East End, and to clinch the matter, to make sure that the whole nation should be completely united, they have gone out of their way to make a deliberate attack upon the Royal Family in Buckingham Palace. With the result that the nation is both angrier and more united than it was before the raids began.

What then has been gained? World opinion—and especially opinion in the United States—has been shocked by these new outrageous tactics. In a few days these people themselves have done more to show the world exactly what kind of people they are than all our propagandists put together could have done in ten years' hard talking. They have, in short, done our work for us. Moreover, if you are going to embark on so momentous a step as the indiscriminate bombing of a great capital city, it is clear that you should have your reasons for taking this step all along one line and ready to be clearly presented. What you cannot do is to wobble between two entirely contradictory sets of reasons. But this is just what the Nazis have done. In one breath they pretend to be setting about this bombing in a mood of mournful reluctance, being driven to adopt "reprisals" for our attacks upon military objectives in Germany. But in the next breath they tell the world that they set about this foul task most gleefully, because they are the tough men, the ruthless aggressors, the new Huns, the grim conquerors of the world, the terrors, who will not brook the least sign of resistance and are ready if necessary to wade through blood to gain their ends.

That, of course, is the truer picture of themselves—except they are not as tough as they'd like us to believe they are—but the point is, one attitude completely cancels out the other. You can't at one and the same time be the reluctant humanitarian and also the ruthless tough, but that is what recent Nazi propaganda asks the world to believe, with the result that the world stares in disbelief and astonishment and begins to wonder what is happening behind the scenes with these people, who used to be much more artful propagandists than this. Again, another complete contradiction has made its appearance. One half of their propaganda—notably

Goebbels himself a day or two ago—is taking the line that Britain is now almost completely disorganised and demoralised—which of course is absolute rubbish—and that her final conquest is merely a matter of another week or two. It is, in fact, a walk over. But the other half of the propaganda now plays down the talk of invasion at all, says it may not even be tried or can be postponed until another year, that the air blockade will be enough, and that you should keep your eye on Egypt and the Italians. This week there has been a lot of this kind of talk from the Nazi propaganda machine. Then again, in minor matters there is the same queer contradiction. At one moment the world is told that the R.A.F. is rapidly losing its power of resistance, and that the Luftwaffe—that same Luftwaffe which lost no less than a hundred and eighty seven 'planes, mostly bombers, on Sunday—is now having it all its own way. Then the next moment it is admitted that the British resistance is very stiff indeed, and will only be broken after considerable sacrifices have been made.

Where are you? It simply doesn't make sense. I'm not, of course, at this late hour trying to find any truth in that mixture of screams, whines, and threats which is supposed to be a statement of the Nazi case, but one does expect to find in the creations of this gigantic lie factory some sort of immediate consistency, some line of attack upon other people's credulity. But here there is nothing but a wild muddle, just as in their actual recent tactics, with their wild and expensive sudden changes of method, there is evidence of haste and bewilderment and a touch of despair. These are not only puzzling but also puzzled men. That flush of victory which they knew just after the collapse of France seems to have completely disappeared. That all-conquering air seems to have left them. Something has gone wrong behind the scenes. Terrible doubts have crept in. The plan, which left them the masters of Europe this year and probably the masters of the world next year—for don't imagine they can ever stop, no matter how great their conquests, for they must go on and on or perish—I say the famous plan seems to have been checked and halted. This does not mean they are now less dangerous. On the contrary, I believe they are more immediately dangerous than ever, ready to stop at nothing, even the loss of hundreds of thousands of lives in an attempt to conquer this island, but on the other hand I do believe that it also means that if they can be held now, seized firmly by the throat, that mad Teutonic fury may suddenly leave them and there may be a gigantic collapse, and the world may wake up one morning to find them gone and feel that it is recovering from an evil dream.

XXXVII. There Is Never a Dull Moment

September 19, 1940

I HAVE DESCRIBED some of the adventures I was
having. Those adventures have continued. There is
never a dull moment here, these days.

Yesterday, having spent most of the day in a film
studio dictating, throughout five or six air-raid warnings, the film story I am working on, I accepted the
invitation of a friend to dine with him at his house in
Mayfair and then spend the rest of the night in his deep
shelter, where he had—oh luxury!—two real beds. I
had not been to bed properly—you know, taking off
your clothes, putting on pyjamas, and getting between
sheets on a spring mattress—since last Saturday night.
I used to be described as a man who looked as if he'd
slept in his clothes. And now I *am* a man who sleeps in
his clothes, and not even in his best clothes, for all my
favourite suits have disappeared in the ruins of that
hotel in which I so carefully unpacked them last Monday. So I accepted with pleasure this invitation to dine
—and afterwards to sleep luxuriously in the deep shelter
—in the grandeur of Mayfair. The evening air-raid
warning—the real thing—went off just before we sat
down to dinner—but we agreed that raid or no raid we
would try to eat our dinner in peace in the dining room.
Which we did with some success, though there was a

[244]

good deal of noise outside. We decided, however, to take our coffee below in the deep shelter, and there we went in a solemn procession, leaving a fine rich trail of cigar smoke. The shelter was all that I had been promised, and there, awaiting my pleasure, was the bed—pillows, sheets, everything, just as I'd remembered beds having. After an hour or so, during which we had some good talk about the world we wanted after this war, about the *real* democracy, economic as well as political and social, that we were beginning to demand, we were reduced to three, but the talk was as brisk as ever.

And then, just when I was beginning to wonder about that bed, for it was now about half-past eleven, and for several nights before I hadn't even started dozing until about three in the morning, there came an urgent message to say that the whole street had been plastered with incendiary bombs, and the upper part of this house and the house next door were now burning. We dashed upstairs to find that this, to say the least of it, was no exaggeration. The whole street appeared to be burning or fizzling. Fire engines were appearing out of nowhere. Little auxiliary firemen—I call them little not out of contempt or patronage, for they were as brave as lions and as industrious as beavers, but just because they actually *were* all little—came dashing in, carrying stirrup pumps and other apparatus. I kept seeing, for he seemed to appear and disappear like magic, a small fierce parson in a tin hat. There was, of course, as usual a dream-like quality about all this experience, which remained even when it became menacing as it very frequently did. I went out into the street, which was now well-lighted by these fires, though one after another were fairly quickly subdued by the fire-fighters and their engines, and immediately every anti-aircraft gun in the world seemed to open out, so that the sky seemed to be filled with bursting stars, and down came the shrapnel and casing like hail. That was bad enough, but what was worse was, after venturing out again—I say *venturing* because not only had I no tin hat, as all these other people had, but I hadn't a hat at all—that I heard a tremendous whistling and rushing, like a little locomotive descending on me, and apparently coming straight for me. I reached the house in three enormous lightning jumps and hastily made myself as small as possible, expecting the bomb somewhere very close. But there was no explosion at all, not a sound, and I do not know where it went or whether it was a dud or a time bomb. Meanwhile fresh fires seemed to start out of nothing in various neighbouring upper storeys, and for a few minutes would glare fiercely but were soon got under control.

After that I appeared to have all manner of fantastic adventures, some of them connected with filling buckets in mysterious upper bathrooms of flats full of smoke and firemen, and others, more sinister still, connected with one of those little narrow house elevators or lifts that you work yourself and that stop and start a good deal on their own and seem uncertain at any time and just a nightmare during an air raid with the roof above them on fire. I gave up the famous bed I had been promised—this was now about three in the morning—to the third member of our little party, a young and dashing member of Parliament who had worked so enthusiastically on the roof as a very auxiliary fireman that he had badly cut both his hands and feet. I made a bed of three long cushions and an eiderdown and flung myself on the floor, for the fourth night in succession, to get some sleep. It did not arrive for some time, as is often the case when one is over-tired, but when at last it did and I was wandering far away in some other and saner world, the lights were flashed on and loud voices arrived with them, telling us that the fires had broken out again and the whole place must be evacuated. It turned out afterwards not to be necessary, though it took us some time to discover that, and then there was just time for some more uneasy dozing before morning. But then there I was, at the breakfast table with my host, drinking excellent coffee and eating kedgeree, glancing at the papers and talking of this and that, with the whole mad burning night gone like a dream.

It's not—let's face it—a good life, and even apart from the danger, there is a constant sense of strain, loss of sleep, slowing down of one's work and so on. But we're doing our work. We're taking it. And if it comes to playing this lunatic game of who can endure the most bombings, if necessary we'll beat them at that too.

I saw a little shop early yesterday morning that had been badly hit. But it was open and there was a notice scrawled up: "Hitler was our last customer. Will you be the next? We're still open." That's the spirit.

XXXVIII. We Await New Developments

September 22, 1940

WE AWAIT new developments. An invasion is still possible, though every week it is postponed makes the attempt a more reckless gamble. Still that is no reason why the Nazis should not attempt it, because they are nothing if not reckless gamblers. It has always been one of the mistakes of their opponents to suppose that these men would not pursue a certain line of action because on the surface such an action appeared to be wildly unreasonable, the maddest gambling. We should always remember that the Nazi leaders are not solemn responsible statesmen of the old school, who if they make a few mistakes can retire comfortably from public office, but far more like gangsters who have to be ready to shoot their way out at a moment's notice. With them it must always be all or nothing, a fact that, combined with their complete lack of ordinary responsibilities and scruples shown in their disregard of other people's lives, gives them a certain immediate advantage. So invasion, though it has ever dwindling prospects of success, is still a possibility, and is undoubtedly being so regarded here, where the preparations to give the visitors a very warm welcome still go forward.

On the other hand, a large-scale combined German-Italian assault upon Gibraltar, Egypt and the Sudan, and the Near East, is just as likely and certainly a rather more hopeful proposition than a trip across these cold rough seas, a trip for which return tickets will not be easily available. We shall see. Here you may show a little impatience, and ask why the initiative should be left to Hitler, why we should merely wait on the defensive. This is a very important question, which demands a very careful answer.

In the first place, even at the present time we are by no means strictly on the defensive, and all this talk of "What will Hitler try next?" should not hide that significant fact. The spectacular air war and all this Nazi propaganda nonsense about blockading Britain should not make us forget that we happen to have a very powerful and efficient Navy, and that that Navy is still doing its work, namely, not only guarding these shores but also strangling the Nazi war economy. The British blockade, though you may not hear much about it, happens to be still in operation. Our ships still sail the high seas, bringing us whatever we need, and German ships stay at home or merely creep along the coast, bringing them nothing. Our shipping losses are not light, but they are still much smaller than they were, merely from U-boat action, during the worst months of the last war, and we have received a great deal of extra shipping from our various allies.

Germany has been able to plunder half Western Europe—and so has been able to postpone a settlement of her food problem—but the fact remains that she is

still becoming increasingly short of essential war materials because the captured countries had no great supplies
of such things. The oil problem is still there, and not
less so because all this aerial activity must be expensive
and the very efficient bombing by the R.A.F. of oil re-
fineries and stores has considerably lowered existing
stocks. In short, our own particular offensive, the silent
and unspectacular pressure of sea power, has continued
without stopping, and even though we may sometimes
overlook that fact you may be sure the German General
Staff and their experts don't forget. It would be just
about as easy as trying to forget a strong hand round
your throat.

But that is not all. We have another offensive that
never stops. That is the bombing offensive of the R.A.F.,
which goes on hitting its targets—factories, railways and
other communications, shipping and troop concentra-
tions—night after night, inflicting tremendous damage.
And not only does this go on unceasingly, but it steadily
increases and will increase enormously, as more and
bigger bombers are brought into action and the longer
nights enable us to travel farther or spend more time
over the targets. Just now, for obvious reasons, the
bombers are concentrating less than usual on targets
within Germany and more on the Channel ports, where
railway sidings, dockyards and basins, transports and
barges—sometimes, it is rumoured, crammed with men
—are nightly being blown to blazes, at a very small cost
to ourselves and at a very considerable cost to the Nazis.

[251]

If they decide to give up the idea of invasion, then the full bomber force is available to attack German factories and transport. This then is the other arm of the offensive that never stops.

So much for the Navy and the Royal Air Force. When we come to the Army, we are dealing with a force that is far smaller than the enemy's and that is being rapidly built and heavily armoured. At the moment it is obvious that the British Army can only be on the defensive, but there could be no bigger mistake than to imagine that its leaders do not see this army as doing anything else but defend. It is being trained to attack. You may ask how it can ever expect to succeed against an army several times its size. As things are at present, it could not hope to succeed anywhere on the continent, but supposing that control of the air, that vital factor, passes into our hands, as it did towards the end of the last war? It has already been shown by the Nazis themselves that mere numbers of men no longer mean everything, that a very heavily armed and swift-moving attacking force, working in cooperation with a superior combination of bombing, fighting and reconnaissance planes, can if necessary smash its way through armies that have an advantage in numbers. Moreover, Germany's hold on the countries she has conquered may easily become more precarious as the situation gets worse and the Nazis make more and more severe demands on the conquered peoples. We know already that the velvet glove of the conqueror is wearing thin and that the people of Norway, Holland, Belgium, France are beginning to feel the iron hand that wears the glove. Two or three summer months of Nazi occupation, with everybody on their best behaviour, is one thing. An autumn and winter of them, with the Nazis no longer on their best behaviour but reverting to type, is quite another thing. Talk about fifth columnists! Germany is faced with the problem of coping with whole populations who are ready to act as fifth columnists. This explains why the Nazis have made such desperate attempts to persuade Western Europe that Britain is the real enemy and that what Hitler wants to do is to establish a new European order free from Britain's influence, though they do not go on to explain that this new order consists of a complete economic domination by Germany and of a political tyranny unequalled in our time.

We may be sure that nobody who was not bought even before the Nazis marched in is likely to be deceived by this talk. And fortunately there are no people less able to play for long the part of sympathetic friend to populations whom not long ago they were murdering by the thousand than the Nazis, who nearly all belong to that unhappy type of human being who overcompensates a deep-seated feeling of inferiority by bragging, swaggering and bullying. It is not unreasonable then for our leaders to feel that when our continued offensives by sea and air have more than counterbalanced the German conquests of this summer, when

[253]

the sea blockade has still further reduced the Nazi war economy and the Royal Air Force, which is already acknowledged to be superior in quality, is at least equal in quantity and so on its way to complete domination, then our land forces, armed with every possible device of swift and terrible assault, should have a fair chance of smashing their way through at one or more points along this vast coastline now held by the Nazis. It should be remembered that for all their tall talk, we know a great deal more about expeditionary forces than the Nazis do. It is an old game for us, but a very new and hazardous one for them, depending as it does upon sea power. Flushed and almost drunk with their lightning successes of the summer, the Nazis, I think, at first failed to see any of this, and there can be little doubt that they imagined that after the collapse of France, a chorus of screams and threats would either reduce Britain to sue for peace or would so paralyse our war effort that we could be easily mastered. But after that a good many things went wrong for them. They found that they were not going to be able to use the French fleet against us. Again, the Italians showed no inclination to sacrifice their fleet either inside the Mediterranean or—after a desperate running of the gauntlet past Gibraltar—outside it. Again, the Nazi threats instead of creating disunity here merely heightened our morale, which in turn vastly increased our war effort. This explains, I think, the curious Nazi tactics of the last month.

I call them "curious" because they suggest, instead of the usual sweeping audacious planning, a hodge-podge of not very happy improvisation. First we have the huge air attacks on our southeastern districts, in an effort to destroy our fighter defences. These attacks fail, because our fighter defences are not broken, and the German losses of machines and trained men are terrific. So then we have the indiscriminate terror bombing of London. Now we have always known that this would happen, but I for one have always held that it would not happen until the Nazis were beginning to feel desperate, and for this reason—that such terror bombing of a huge helpless civilian population would produce such instant revulsion of feeling throughout the world, and especially in the United States, that it was useless to try it except as a last desperate throw of the dice. Moreover, by bombing every quarter of the capital, from the poorest parts of the East End to Buckingham Palace itself, the Nazis have only heightened, if anything, the strong feeling of national unity, and the net result, apart from some obvious inconvenience, strain, and some personal tragedies, has been to leave our war effort where it found it, and to make the mass of the people more angry and determined than ever. Behind all this too has been a strange confused propaganda, contradicting itself at every turn, and suggesting that Goebbels' organisation could not be given a definite line to work along because no such line existed.

Only two months ago, these people, who had over-run almost all Western Europe, were sitting on top of the world. All was to be over in a few weeks. There were dates announced for the dictating of peace and the triumphal marches. But now they are reduced to trying one desperate move after another, and hurriedly sacrificing valuable men, machines and material, rushing here and there for hasty conferences, now still pretending that they will have won the war in another week or two, now admitting that after all it may be a long and hard conflict. You must admit this is a very strange transformation, suggesting that something has gone badly wrong behind the scenes. Meanwhile, I repeat, we await new developments.

XXXIX. Going North

September 24, 1940

I AM GOING north for a week or two, back to my
native Yorkshire. I'm not getting out of London
because there are too many bombs for me, though I
have had my adventures with them, and so contrived
my existence last week that for five days I never succeeded in getting my clothes off and reaching the inside
of a bed. If I thought the bombing of London would
be intensified, I would stay on, but my own feeling is—
and so far events have borne me out—that the bombing
is decreasing in weight and violence. Therefore as it
does not seem likely that there will be anything new to
report about the London scene during the next week or
two, I thought I would take this opportunity of doing
what I've wanted to do for the last two months, that is
to go up north, to that other and quite different half of
England, to get some idea of what is happening there
and how the people, who are responsible, of course, for
most of our heavy industries, are taking it all.

It would be a surprise to the Nazi airmen we have
captured recently to learn that I proposed to go north,
for it appears that they have been told—and solemnly
believe—that industrial northern England is completely
under Nazi domination. This is merely one of the new
German fairy tales with which these young men are

now being lulled into a false security. They have been told that hundreds of thousands of German troops have invaded England and Ireland, and that the whole of Scotland has been captured by troops landed from Norway. The Royal Family and the Government, they are told, are now besieged in London, and only this southeast corner of England is still in British hands. In addition, some of them believe that the whole of the British Fleet has been sunk, that Portsmouth is almost a German naval base, and that even in London great riots and demonstrations in favour of peace are taking place day and night. The end, according to this new fairy tale, is in sight. The starving British people are waiting to welcome the victorious Nazis. So they are, but in another sense. The British people, of course, aren't starving, and the Nazis equally aren't victorious. But that our people are waiting to welcome the Nazis whenever they arrive is true enough. They will receive such a welcome as they've never had before, and it will be all the more surprising because they are being fed with such lying dope as this.

I must repeat that the Nazis, for people who have just had a series of lightning conquests, are now behaving in a strangely suspicious manner. What is the point of telling their people—even the very men called upon to fight—all this ridiculous nonsense? It is not merely a matter of touching up the facts, but of persuading their fighting men to believe the most monstrous lies, all calculated to persuade them that the war is won except for some small effort that they have to make during the next day or two. I can see the point of trying to persuade your opponent that all is over with him—which is the trick the Nazis worked with some success in France and Belgium—but to persuade your own fighting men that all is nearly over, when you know that at any moment they may be called upon to begin a long and weary campaign, suggests that these men have lost heart and need the most fantastic restoratives.

It is true that these young Nazi pilots we capture, who discover to their astonishment that Britain is not starving, is armed to the teeth, and ready if necessary to fight for years, cannot return to tell their comrades the truth, cannot spread their sudden disillusionment. And yet I would have thought that juggling with lies of these gigantic dimensions is like playing with an enormous boomerang, which at any moment may return and knock you flat. A government that exhibited such an obvious contempt for my intelligence would soon lose my allegiance, for I would feel that it had not only been misleading me but downright insulting me. And here are an air force and army that in a few weeks completely over-ran half Western Europe, and yet now, only a month or two later, it has to be fed with the soothing syrup of such colossal lies. Why? What has happened to these soldiers and airmen? And what has happened to the civilian population behind them? And, more important still, what has happened to the Nazi leaders that they take the risk of all their people being so horribly disillusioned and they themselves made to look like fools? Even Goebbels himself would find it hard to conjure a Britain almost at the mercy of invading Nazi forces back into a Britain that is completely untouched and has never seen a Nazi invader. Does it mean that the Nazis are changing their plans, and making use of any nonsense as a cover for that change, or does it mean that now they feel committed to an attempt at invasion?

If so, the question of transport must be giving them a headache. One of our military experts has been working out the problem for them. He estimates that to transport a mechanised force of 100,000 men with the minimum of heavy equipment, a nice little armada of from 1,300 to 1,500 large flat-bottomed barges would be required. This number would be necessary merely to convey the 100,000 men and their equipment across the sea, but of course that is only the beginning of the problem, for they would have to be supplied regularly with ammunition and supplies. To assemble 1,300 to 1,500 of such boats or barges, then to move them across the sea, at a speed of probably not more than eight knots, in face of our air force and the most powerful navy in the world, will be quite a task, even if wind and weather be favourable; and even then, if by some miracle of organisation this part of the greater task is accomplished without a loss of more than half the vessels and the men and equipment they carry, they have still to be landed bang in the face of an army that has been waiting for them—and how!—ever since Dunkirk. Again, our expert estimates that for a seven days' mobile campaign, even this force of 100,000 men would require for its tanks and other vehicles something like 2,750,000 gallons of petrol, all of which have also to be transported across the sea. And all this for a force of only 100,000 men, that is of five mechanised divisions with corps and army troops. But in order to over-run Poland, which had most of its air force put out of action in the first twenty-four hours, it took no less than 37 infantry divisions, 5 motorised divisions, 5 armoured divisions, 4 light mechanised divisions, and many tank regiments. To bring even a fraction of such a force across the sea would demand the most gigantic armada of vessels. Yet obviously anything less than such a force and at least such an equipment would stand no chance whatever against our own heavily mechanised armies, all specially trained by this time to repel invaders on ground now familiar to them and quite unfamiliar to the attacking forces.

Well, they may try it, for they are nothing if not gamblers. But I am going north, for I feel there is nothing more at the moment I can report about life in London under the air raids. I have paid my tribute to the grand resolution and courage of the great city of my adoption and all its folk—especially the women and girls—not only the mothers and housewives, but the hundreds of thousands of nurses, secretaries, clerks, shop-girls, waitresses, who've turned up morning after morning, still trim and smiling, if a little weary, and who've defied Goering and all his air force. I can say nothing new, so I feel it is time I went back to my own folk in the north, to see what life is like up there, among the mills and the moors. Don't imagine that they haven't had their share of the bombing. They have not had the continued determined attack upon their *morale* that the Londoners have had, but they've heard the bombers droning and the bombs thudding and roaring, and stared at the ruins next morning.

It will at least be interesting to see how the air-raid life is being lived in other and smaller cities, where it has not yet developed into a kind of grim routine as it has now in London. The change up north will be less dramatic, for life is much grimmer up there, among the tall chimneys and the grey stone walls, at any time, and you might say that industry has been waging a kind of blitzkrieg up there for generations. Actually, I suppose that from the point of view of our war effort, I am going from the less important to the more important region, for though London is the capital of our wide commonwealth, the seat of government, the centre of all our financial interests, it is, after all, not the place where the machinery and materials of war are made. Moreover, both industrial Yorkshire and Lancashire have groups of towns—and you can't tell where one ends and the next begins—that together make up centres of population as great as London itself. In fact, Britain could still wage this war even if London had become uninhabitable, which it is, of course, far from being at the moment, except for the faint-hearted. But Britain without the industrial north, where the factories go on endlessly, would be in a sorry state. And the north is almost a different country, with quite a different outlook from London and the south. It always has its point of view. What that point of view is at the moment I don't know, but with any luck I soon will.

2